Linda Milburn
2003

Joanne Nuchardt

MW00935883

FULLY ALIVE

Also published in the Saybrook
"Human Future" Series:

My Quest for Beauty, by
Rollo May

*American Politics and
Humanistic Psychology,*
by Rollo May,
Carl Rogers and Others

Nobel Prize Conversations,
by Sir John Eccles,
Roger Sperry, Ilya Prigogine,
Brian Josephson and Norman Cousins

ROY LAURENS

SAYBROOK

San Francisco   Dallas   New York

Quotations from copyrighted poetry and prose are noted in an "Acknowledgments" section at the end of the volume.

Copyright © 1985 by Saybrook Publishing Company

All rights reserved. No part of this work may be reproduced or transmitted in any form or by any means, electronic or mechanical, including photocopying and recording, or by any information storage and retrieval system, except as may be expressly permitted by the 1976 Copyright Act or in writing from the publisher. To request permission, write: Saybrook Publishing Company, 3518 Armstrong Avenue, Dallas, TX 75205

Designed by Alison Esposito and Chiles & Chiles

Library of Congress Cataloging-in-Publication Data

Laurens, Roy, 1921–
  Fully alive.

  1. Cerebral dominance.   2. Brain—Localization of
functions.   3. Intellect.   4. Mind and body.   I. Title.
QP385.5.L38   1985   150   85-61686
ISBN 0-933071-03-5

Saybrook Publishing Company
3518 Armstrong Avenue, Dallas, TX 75205
Printed in the United States of America
Distributed by W. W. Norton & Company
500 Fifth Avenue
New York, New York 10110

To my dear wife
and children

A Word of Thanks

Dr. Roger Sperry, Nobel Laureate, and Dr. Donald Polkinghorne, president of the Saybrook Institute, provided the inspiration for much of the research upon which this book is based. The genesis of much of the phenomenological and semantic basis for the book derives from the Reverend Dr. Webster Kitchell Howell. Drs. William T. Moore, Robert Giles, James Hall and William Tedford kindly consented to check the manuscript for me. Of course, none of the above is responsible in any way for the contents of the book. Nathan Mitchell, senior editor of the Saybrook Publishing Company, made the book possible, and Frank O'Connor was the production editor.

A special word of thanks is due those persons who have assisted me in my research. While this book is based on actual experiences, the people depicted in it must remain anonymous. My chief concern is to preserve the human rights of the participants, both in my clinical practice and in my research. I want all those who have been associated with me to know that our experiences within the therapeutic or research environment are—and will continue to be—inviolate.

Roy Laurens

CONTENTS

Introduction

by James Hall, M.D., past president of the Isthmus In-stitute, author of Clinical Use of Dreams, Jungian Dream Interpretation, *and (with Harold Crasilneck)* Clinical Hypnosis.

Dr. Laurens's *Fully Alive* is quite possibly the most important book to have come into my hands in many years. This remarkable work is a significant indicator of a fundamental revolution in human science and in human living. It is moreover a profound theoretical insight into *personal* scientific experimental technique, presenting aspects of human science which can and should be a part of everyone's life.

If you embark successfully on the journey suggested by the personal experiments in *Fully Alive,* you will find yourself not simply changing habits or attitudes (these are, anyway, constructions of our rational identities) but changing at a far deeper, non-rational and non-conscious level. As that deep change occurs, you will find yourself naturally and spontaneously drawn toward a healthier approach to such practical matters as diet, exercise, weight control, smoking and professional relationships. For example, the record kept by "Tom," a subject in Dr. Laurens's research experiments, will vividly demonstrate this kind of change as you move from chapter to chapter in the book.

Dr. Laurens tells his story as a scientist and as a very human man. The reader walks with him through his search for a larger experience, one that leads to an expansion of reality far beyond his dreams. *Fully Alive* is at once a wonderful personal story, an important contribution to the growing literature on the deeper nature of the mind, and a clear and simple guide to awakening potentials for achievement in business, health and personal relationships.

When Freda, a beautiful teenager, is brought to him for

help, Dr. Laurens embarks on a healing journey which leads to Freda's amazing recovery and then, later, to a new wholeness in himself and those clients who participate with him in his experiments.

Fully Alive awakens the need for change in a way that distinguishes it from the dozens of self-help, do-it-yourself books that flood the market today. Most of the literature in the self-help genre—from diet plans to jogging manuals—appeals to that rational, self-conscious identity which seeks to preserve itself at all costs against the inevitable process of aging, illness, disappointment and loss. Rules and regulations replace free, full living, with the frequent result that the harder one's rational mind struggles to control eating, exercise, emotions, etc., the less satisfying—and less permanent—the outcome is.

The experiments in this book will help you discover how to fully *feel* your feelings and then let go of them without getting caught up in the harmful psychological defenses of repression or acting out. The secret, as Dr. Laurens notes, is the willingness to live fully with all you are and can be. To live only in the controlled, carefully orchestrated world of the rational mind is to live, at best, a half-life half-humanly.

At a conference chaired by me at the Isthmus Institute in Dallas, Dr. Roger Sperry, 1981 Nobel Laureate in physiology/medicine, called attention to some reasons why science, philosophy and religion have heretofore been unsuccessful in their quests for human definition. Sperry demonstrated first that non-material intentions exert a "downward" causal control over the material electro-chemical activities of the human brain. Secondly, Sperry and others have implied that *more than one kind* of mental organization is at work in human beings.

Combining these insights with results of his own research, Roy Laurens has taken the entire issue a critical step further. What makes us human, Laurens argues in *Fully Alive,* is not merely the rational mind, remarkable as it is, but *two minds* which coexist in human beings but in no other species. Two linked but distinct forms of mental organization, each one processing our experience in a specialized way, inhabit that bundle of energies and potentials we call the "human person."

That "other" mind, unlike its rational partner, neither speaks in sentences, nor analyzes, nor is conscious of itself. It is a mind wholly bound to body and to its environment—bound, indeed to *all* of space and time from life's evolutionary origins to its present multiple and complex forms. Laurens calls it variously "super-animal," "holistic," "healing," "nurturing." It is not simply another function of our rational, self-conscious identities, nor is it an appendix, inert and relatively useless, left over from eons of evolution. It is a *real* mind, as essential for human health and wholeness as the self-consciously intelligent mind which struggles to preserve our rational identities and fears losing control over our life and environment.

But Laurens does not merely assert the existence of another mind, nor does he ask readers to accept it on "good scientific authority." Laurens invites you to conduct your own personal experiments to discover for yourself the existence of that other mind which binds us to all time and all space in our evolving universe. You are asked not only to share his research, but to create and participate in your own. In this book, *you* are the scientist, testing, probing, keeping your own records and measurements, sifting through your own cumulative experiments to discover what's true and what isn't.

Fully Alive suggests a way out of that cul-de-sac to which a great deal of modern science and philosophy has led. It avoids the materialist fallacy that tries to reduce humankind to the operations of quantum physics and at the same time does not resort to mystical hocus-pocus. Dr. Laurens grounds the existence of the "other" mind, conscious-bound to all time, on the same basis of biological evolution, which has developed a chain of life forms that link the simplest proto-cells to more complex bilateral organisms, to highly sophisticated, bilateral and brain-endowed humans.

Fully Alive is not a comfortable book, but it is an exciting book, as engrossing as a novel. Reaching beyond the limits of language, it will challenge, surprise, irritate and tease. With the viewpoint that informs this book we seem to be approaching a breakthrough that overcomes classical conflicts between "matter" and "spirit," mind and brain, "reason" and "emotion." *Fully Alive* outlines an approach to health and human living that goes beyond the so-called "crises" of identity. For ultimately, your ego-identity is precisely that aspect of you which most likely will *not* survive, either in the ego-transformations of *this* life or in any postmortem existence. What may survive of us is precisely that bound mental organization, enfolding all of our evolutionary time, while transcending its material limits. That mind, selfless, self-sacrificing and "spiritual," has intimate, immediate knowledge of a love stronger than death. It never calls attention to itself, nor does it register imperious demands. It is, to cite a poem of Wallace Stevens, as silent as Plato's ghost or Aristotle's skeleton . . . incapable of speaking. Yet it is *that* mind which portends us, makes us *possible.* It will love us unconditionally, nourish us and cherish us, never leave us alone—if we are willing to let it in. Perhaps it will reincarnate us again in new forms.

This book provides you with a revolutionary, personal, scientific, experimental technique which does not require you to change a single thing about your living—but invites you to change the foundations of your whole life. I highly recommend it.

I shall be telling this with a sigh
Somewhere ages and ages hence:
Two roads diverged in a wood, and I—
I took the one less travelled by,
And that has made all the difference.

Robert Frost

Among the questions disputed by modern brain researchers is "Do humans have a mind separate from the brain?" Are there real mental activities distinct from the electro-chemical functions of the brain? Scientists of a materialist bent have answered these questions negatively. For them, mind is simply an "effect" produced by the brain's complex chemical reactions; it has no separate existence, no distinct reality of its own.

But recent research into the mind/brain relationship repudiates the older materialist view. *Fully Alive* has grown out of this newer research, but it is not a technical work on the subject of "split brain" experiments. I have written *Fully Alive* for the non-specialist reader who wants to experience the human potential for wholeness and healing. Such an experience is possible only if we recognize that humans have not only *a* mind distinct from brain, but *two* minds distinct from each other and both necessary for a full, healthy life.

My conviction that we humans have *two* minds may seem startling, but it is supported by contemporary research on the subject. For a long time scientists have known that the human brain is formed of a right and a left hemisphere. We now know that each of the two brain halves processes its electro-chemical signals in completely different ways. The left hemisphere processes the signals in a rational, linear sequence, while the right hemisphere processes them in self-emergent whole patterns. These two mental organizations do not reflect each other.

Nobel Laureate Roger Sperry's recent research, and that of fellow Laureate Sir John Eccles, has shown that real mental intentions and ideas—separate and distinct from the brain—truly exist. Indeed, Eccles demonstrated that such mental intentions initiate the burst of electro-chemical discharges in the brain which lead to voluntary motor activities. Combining Sperry's and Eccles's work, we are left with the inescapable conclusion that humans have not only one mind that acts, through choice and decision, upon the brain, but *two* minds which exhibit quite different modes of processing our experience.

Our two minds are not, however, identified with the brain's two hemispheres. Rather, our having two hemispheres created the *potential* for having another mind. This potential was implicit in the very origins of life. For as soon as the simplest single-celled animal appeared in the course of evolution, a "boundary" was created between it and reality outside it. In the human species this boundary became conscious through the emergence of our rational minds, which permit us to step back from our experience and reflect on it.

Such, very briefly sketched, is the background and scientific basis for what follows in *Fully Alive*.

I

TIME

The Girl Who Discovered Time

    Freda was in her late teens, a blond with those ice blue eyes which seem almost transparent. She had come in with the social worker and was standing in front of my desk. Then I noticed what had seemed transparency in her eyes was actually emptiness. I was looking through two holes into nothing. There was no mind connected to this lovely body.

"Sit down, Freda," the social worker said. She sat down. "Your skirt is hiked up, Freda." She pulled it down.

I was reading Freda's file. She had been in an automobile accident seven months before. Her body had been hurled through the windshield of her own car and then through the windshield of the truck which had hit her head-on. Since then she had had no memory of who she was, nor was she able to remember any sequence of events which had just happened.

"Where are the X-rays?," I asked.

"Uh, aren't they here?" The social worker was smoothing Freda's collar. "Where is your list, Freda?"

"List?" Freda looked puzzled.

"It's in your hand, Freda." The social worker put the list on my desk. "You see we're working on basic things— dressing, keeping our clothes neat, trying to remember our name." I looked at the list. They were using behavior-modification techniques to train this body sitting before me so that she would cause the minimum trouble in a care routine.

I came around the desk and carefully felt her cranium. There was no indication of trauma left. "Will you see if you can find the X-rays, please?" (I knew they wouldn't show anything.)

As the social worker left, I sat on the edge of my desk in front of Freda. Such a pretty girl, a sensitive-looking face, but her mind was not connected to it. How ultimately horrible. I could feel terror rising and overwhelming me. I was kneeling on the floor with her hands in mine saying, "I'm so sorry; I'm so sorry. . . ."

"They left me in the car," Freda said, "Mommy and Daddy left me in the car."

"Car? What car?" I realized she was not talking about the accident she had just suffered. Her voice had the accent of a young child. I later learned Freda had begun speaking of an incident which happened when she was four years old, travelling in a car with her parents. "Uh. . . . why don't you . . ."

"I'm strapped in. I can't reach, don't know how to open the door."

"Can you see where your mommy and daddy are going?"

"I can't see over the door except the sky. I want to see Grandpa. They've left me. I'm crying and crying." She *was* crying. She looked at me. Two tiny blue sparks flamed at the back of her eyes.

When the social worker finally came back with the X-rays, Freda was sitting up in the chair, blue eyes blazing, showering me with a torrent of words about how she had been mistreated by her parents. The social worker caught what was happening. She gently closed the door and left. Freda and I were left in her four-year-old world. That was how we began our discovery of time. And it was through discovering time that we were able to find her mind—in fact, her *two* minds.

Human Science

There were two points of view about Freda's condition when she came into my office. The common scientific view was that mind is a word for brain, that if Freda had no "mind" it was because the brain was damaged and couldn't function.

I had a different point of view. As a result of my own research and that of others, I believed (no, I knew) that Freda's mind ordered her brain, not the other way around. It was possible that her brain was functional but that it had become disconnected from her mind, i.e. from the higher patterns of her mental organization. If I had simply followed the common scientific view and assumed brain damage, I could have looked for improved behavior to the extent that the brain healed itself. This course of treatment would have used behavior modification, similar to what was being done by the social worker, to train Freda to live within the range of her brain's recovery.

Then an astonishing thing happened. As Freda sat before me, I felt myself pulled toward the realization that this girl not only still had her mind but that her mind was active and lively. The problem was that Freda's mind dwelled in a time that was real but different from the time showing on the clock above the desk in my office. *I found myself alive in a room where two worlds of time—each real, though different—existed simultaneously.*

I had no choice. There was only one thing to do: to travel with Freda into a time I knew nothing about and leave behind the time showing on my office clock.

In short, I chose to go a less travelled road with Freda. I committed myself to living with her fully wherever and whenever she was. If Freda's time was the time of her four-year-old world, I would join her there, and we would be fully alive in that world.

One might think that Freda was obsessed by the past. No. She was living in a vivid world that truly existed for her and me. Freda's experiences as an unhappy four-year-old strapped in a car and left alone were not just memories. She was really living them, in her real world, all the way.

The critical moment came when Freda was able to identify and connect the two cars that had caused her such emotional and physical anguish: her parents' car, when she was four years old, and the car of her head-on collision. When she made that identification she screamed and fainted.

From that point on, a path of recovery opened up for Freda. Slowly she became able to live in the world of her car crash as well as in her four-year-old world. There was nothing else, just these two worlds fifteen years apart in time. But what time? For Freda *both* worlds were her life, and each demanded that she live *fully* in it. Time wasn't working in Freda's life the way our rational minds say it does—or should. Logic says the past just slips away, disappears, ceases to exist. But Freda knew better. She was discovering that her real life in the present embraced—enfolded—*all* the times of her life. Her four-year-old world, the world of a crying unhappy child, was as real and immediate as the hideous world of her head-on collision. Though it sounds illogical and impossible, Freda found herself fully alive in two worlds of time at once.

The fifteen years in between were eventually filled in, and Freda is now a vivacious nineteen-year-old. What is particularly rewarding to me is that she has retained a sense that all the times of her life are real and belong to her whole existence. She uses her times fully and is beginning to experience being fully alive, a grace to all who know her. The implications of my having lived in all of Freda's times with her were staggering to me. We had discovered a time which enfolded all the experiences of her life but which continued to exist after specific events in her life had passed.

I began to wonder if Freda's discovery of time might provide a key to exploring a hidden potential of the mind—one which, if discovered and used, could lead to a life fuller than I had ever imagined possible. That is how my quest for living fully began. I had been a scientist for forty years. Now I became a detective, a seeker after clues. Questions—many doubts—came pouring in on me. Was some kind of "mind" tucked away in Freda's experience of being alive in two worlds of time at once? Had Freda stumbled onto a reality which I, a research scientist with all the academic credentials, had never bothered to notice? Would I have to surrender some of my own theories about what "mind" is and how it works?

So I began my quest—a detective and a doubter.

The Discovery of Mind in Time

From the beginning of history, I knew, human beings have acknowledged the existence of mind. Our ancestors, remote and proximate, have prized it, recognized its reality and relied on its ideas, ideals and intuitions. When I was an undergraduate at Princeton many years ago, my professors diligently pointed out how rich the ancient languages were in words to express the subtle, layered activities usually rendered by the single word "mind" in English. Latin knew not only *mens* (whence English "mental"), but also *intellectus, ratio, anima animus, appetitus* (used to convey the mind's rigorous search for truth as well as the body's hungry appetite). Greek was similarly rich in its repertoire of expressions for mental activity: *nous* (the "mind" in English words like "noumenal"), *psychē* (often translated "soul," but used, interestingly, to form English "psychology"), *phrēn* "mind," (giving rise to a word of nearly opposite meaning in English, "frenzy").

I used to smile at the clumsiness of the Greeks and Romans who couldn't hit upon a compact four-letter word—like mind—to say what they meant. With Freda's help I have learned better. We scientists have never been able to measure mind, to see, touch, feel or hear it. In short, until recently mind has resisted all experiments aimed at giving it an exact quantitative definition. And since science sometimes assumes that what can't be measured doesn't exist, doubts about the scientific reality of a mind independent from the brain still exist. The question has been, "If I cut off your head, where is your mind?"

Doubts, however pervasive, do not constitute demonstrations of truth or fact. When it comes to the issue of mind, you are as well equipped as any scientist to raise questions and propose answers. I have had to face the fact that neither my education nor my academic credentials have been sufficient to find human truth. What is needed is the experience of life and the world. Calling upon your deepest human experience ask yourself, "Is my mind more than my brain?"

These are the things I would say are needed for research into the human mind:

(1) Passionate devotion to discovering truth about our own personal mental experiences with the courage to push those experiences all the way until we know we are fully alive.

(2) Openness to receive what this experience teaches us, even if it conflicts with our preconceived views of what "should" be true.

(3) The best use of the best tools for discovering truth and for grasping the disclosures offered by experience.

Arguments may arise about "best tools," but in the case of human mind, you have the finest ones available—yourself, your experience, your mind. The human nervous system is our best research tool.

Often we assume that being scientific means being technical or obscure. This is not so. Science is an attitude of openness to knowledge, a frame of mind, a fearless mode of discovering not only what is but what can *become*, of relating that discovery to our shared experience of being-human. All of us are equipped for these tasks.

Suppose that you could see into the deepest part of a scientist's being and asked, "Do you believe that mind exists, that you exist in some way other than your brain and body?" Surely the answer would be, "Yes, I believe my mind does exist—I just can't find a way to talk about its existing apart from my head."

In trying to talk about the mind's existence, philosophy

came into being—and that long before science. Indeed, the oldest human question deals with the relation between mind and matter. Recently, some scientists have begun paying close attention to this question, and have reached the point of being able to talk about mind without trying to reduce it to brain-parts, chemical substances or electrical currents.

Reach up and touch the top of your head. Some of us have heads that are pointed, and can actually feel a bony protrusion. If you can't, you can still sense where the top of your head is.

I happen to have a bony protrusion. Underneath it is a small part of my brain which initiates voluntary movements, such as shaking a finger or moving the hand, by responding to commands from a non-material source—*our thoughts and mental intentions*. We scientists are discovering that *non-material* reality—what we have commonly called "mind"—initiates *material* events in our brains and bodies.

Thought Experiment

Try this thought experiment with me. I will take the most simple mental act I can think of. Suppose it's changing the position of my finger. I decide to move my finger and then watch it move.

Now I decide to move that finger again, but I don't look

at it this time. Yet I know it moved. A message went from somewhere to my finger and came back to somewhere.

I follow that electro-chemical message along my nerves, up through my spinal column and into my brain. Is this electro-chemical feeling the same as the decision to move my finger? I know it isn't. See how you feel about it.

We know that the simplest voluntary movements (like moving a finger) require that a complex pattern of nerve impulses be activated in the human brain. Are these nerve impulses the same thing as my decision to move a finger? No. The decision comes first, before any neural activity begins. So we have to try to explain the relation between the decision to move the finger, the brain's nerve impulses, and the voluntary movement itself.

The explanation leads us back to thinking about that bony protrusion at the top of our heads. If we measure the radiation coming from our head, we discover that the first nerve impulses are registered in that area at the top of the head. But this registering—and the neural activity that follows—occurs only because, *first,* I made a *mental* decision to move my finger. My *mind's* decision, in other words, activates the first nerve impulses that lead to movement. It isn't the brain that produces my decision; rather, my *decision* prompts the brain into activity.

Once more I decide to move my finger; only this time I imagine that it has been cut off. Still, the *decision* to move the finger still exists. This is known as the phantom limb phenomenon. People who have lost a finger still register, in the mind, the reality of that finger. In mental time, the kind Freda and I discovered, that finger still exists and will continue existing. As Eudora Welty said, in *The Optimist's Daughter,*

> It is memory that is the somnambulist. It will come back in its wounds from across the world, ... calling us by our names and demanding its rightful tears. It will never be impervious. The memory can be hurt, time and again—but in that may lie its final mercy. As long as it's vulnerable to the living moment, it lives for us, and while it lives, and while we are able, we can give it up its due.

Memory—the kind that lives fully in our bodies—is one dimension of that time Freda found, a time which enfolds all that is and has been.

As scientists learn more, it becomes clear that brain cannot explain mind. The brain is not some machine governed by immutable, natural laws of the universe. It does not, blindly following these laws, cause natural patterns of radiation through the brain. No, a very small area of the brain at the top of our heads responds to mental decisions, and its radiation initiates those complex neural patterns which cause the muscles to contract and the finger to move.

One may say, "Big deal! Before, I had a big brain causing my mind; now I have a tiny brain causing my mind." That's just the point. As long as it was a big, complicated brain, scientists could say, "Well, we can't exactly explain how the brain causes the mind, but the brain is so complex that, some day, we'll find a complicated way of convincing you that your mind is nothing more than computerized neuronal interchanges."

Scientists can no longer say that. The part of the brain that initiates voluntary movements is so small that we can comprehend its neuronal traffic. And this traffic does not in any way explain even a simple decision such as changing the position of one's finger.

The Forces of Mind

The finger whose position we have decided to move is made up of countless electrons dancing around nuclei that are composed of subatomic particles. Science has isolated these particles by subjecting them to unimaginable forces of focused energy in cyclotrons. And science has assumed that the laws of quantum mechanics, which appear to govern the behavior of such particles, can explain everything about the finger, its physical structure and its movement.

Does quantum mechanics, however, really explain

everything? Does it explain the *decisions* to move the finger?

Try moving your finger once again. While watching it move, consider that you have also moved its subatomic particles. By the simplest mental decision you have moved those particles further than the world's most powerful cyclotrons can. Make another decision and board a plane to fly around the world. You could, by still another mental decision, slice the bit of tissue which embeds a particular atom of your finger and send it on one of the Voyager space probes to visit Mars, Jupiter, Neptune, Pluto and on out into the farthest reaches of the universe. None of these decisions can be explained by quantum mechanics.

Immutable quantum laws do not control the universe nor do they control you.

Consider, that the atom in the slice from your finger was encompassed in a cell which moved it around regardless of quantum mechanics. The cell is encompassed in a muscle which moves it around. The muscle is encompassed in a network of nerves which move it around. That neural network is encompassed in patterns of neural activity which are encompassed in patterns of more complex neural activity. But mind is not in the neural cell firings. It is the patterns of activity themselves which are the mind. Mind is those non-material patterns mediated through that bony protrusion under the top of your skull.

These patterns encompass this configuration of the universe which is you moving your finger.

Enfolding Time

While quantum mechanics can describe the movement of the subatomic particles in your finger, it cannot explain your decision to move those particles in a trip around the world. Human decisions cannot be reduced to quantum laws, because the mind is more than their reality and encompasses in time the neuronal activity of the brain. This encompassing, by which mind organizes and directs the brain's activity at the subatomic, atomic and molecular levels, is what I call the *enfolding* power of mind. And the mind itself is encompassed—*enfolded*—by the fundamental reality of the evolving universe, the irreversible arrow of time.

Think, then, of all the patterns of order involved in moving your finger. Think of the different patterns in your cells encompassing the ordered movements of your subatomic particles. Think how your muscles encompass their cells and how your brain encompasses the muscles which move your finger, and how your mind enfolds it all. Each level of patterned order acts within the encompassing order of a higher level.

Arthur Koestler called this kind of order "holonarchy"

rather than hierarchy. All are connected, but each lower level could exist without the next higher one.

The nature of *time* explains why this is so. The universe goes in only one direction; it never repeats itself, or goes backward. The experiments you tried a short while ago, when you changed the position of your finger, have already happened. Yet these experiments have not simply disappeared. They continue to exist—but how?

The answer to this question can be found in the *quality of time* which Freda and I discovered. Time does not simply move forward; as it moves, it *enfolds* all that has ever happened. Time constantly *becomes*—and as it becomes, it enfolds the whole evolving history of our universe.

Consider what was involved when you moved your finger. Think of your internal decision, your intention, all the muscles and nerve patterns involved, the air displaced, the heat generated. At the level of self-consciousness you were probably aware of only your finger movement. Paradoxically, it is the self-conscious awareness that will pass away. All else remains. For ultimately, what "caused" the movement was neither neural activity nor conscious awareness, but your mental intention to move the finger. The *intention* is what remains. For our intentions are themselves encompassed—"enfolded"—by the highest level, cosmic mind. God does indeed regard every fallen sparrow, every hair that turns white. In our time-enfolded, mind-enfolded universe, nothing and no one is ever lost.

Time and Mind

Freda's experience—and perhaps your own experiments with finger movement—suggest that there is a time in our lives which doesn't disappear into the past. A superb musical performance—of Bartok's "Concerto for Orchestra," for example—continues existing even after the last note has died away. Not for nothing do we speak of such performances as "unforgettable" or "immortal."

Or think of a room long inhabited by someone deeply loved. A real presence remains there, one as intense as when the loved one still lived. Glenway Wescott, in "The Odor of Rosemary," writes:

> Now and then, an incident suggests how one may be able to perpetuate at least a part of the life of people whom one has known well and long, observed closely and with sensitivity intensified for some reason: by recording a little uniqueness, an uninventable trait or fact. I have had that lady's sweetness in my mind for twenty-five years, two hundred years (more or less) after her death and entombment. It is a beginning of immortality.

Are such experiences genuine, or are they merely tricks we play on ourselves? This book is meant to be a way of finding out.

The universe started with the "big bang" at a tiny point. There is still a residual background of radiation in the universe connected with black holes, which may be the original radiation of the big bang. As time moved forward, new life forms emerged. Hydrogen atoms clotted together to form other kinds of atoms, molecules, suns, worlds and us. Yet the original creation, the "big bang," still exists enfolded within these successive changes and becomings.

Still, time is a reality we measure. The measure of time derives from the movement of the heavenly bodies, night and day, the waxing and waning of the moon. But these movements are slowing down, changing like everything else in the universe. They are always *becoming,* never static.

Scientific measurement, however, needs static time, i.e., it needs an absolute, unchanging standard against which to measure change. Scientists now use atomic clocks which measure the vibration of certain atoms. But on a cosmic scale, since the big bang, vibrations of atoms have also been changing and becoming. To their dismay, scientists are discovering that there is no "atomic clock," either.

The Illusion of "Now"

Classical science, beginning with Aristotle's *Ta Physica,* divided time into past, present and future. These were thought of as absolutes which did not change. Einstein realized there was no such thing as past, present, future, there was no "now" in which we lived. Einstein discovered that "now" was an illusion through his mathematical intuitions. Freda discovered this illusion of "now" through living beyond it. Freda also went beyond Einstein's discovery by experiencing her life as a flux of becoming, always enfolding a kind of "past" which never went away.

We can all break through past-present-future ourselves. In fact, we do it all the time. We have an inner sense of growing older, of changing in all kinds of ways. Freda discovered time in a more dramatic way, but we can all feel a sense in which we are everything we have ever been. The flow of change has not been interrupted to create a "now."

This brings us back to the notion of becoming. Imagine there is no clock; imagine there is no time past, time present, time future. We and the universe are patterns of change. We are becoming and in that becoming we must encompass everything that has ever been. The original background radiation of the big bang, all the atoms, all the evolution of life is encompassed and enfolded by us. We are the stuff of stars. It was not sheer romantic sen-

timent that led the English poet Gerard Manley Hopkins
to exclaim,

> Look at the stars! look, look up at the skies!
> O look at all the fire-folk sitting in the air!

From this point of view consider another scientific idea,
which we all accept without thinking about it, the idea
(entropy) that everything in the universe is running down,
like a top left spinning until friction and gravity cause it
to slow, wobble, then stop. We've all accepted this idea
for so long—yet it applies to only a few rationally isolated
cases. Look around you. Since the random chaos of the
big bang, things have not in fact been running down; they
have been becoming more patterned and complex. Visi-
ble all around you is the self-emerging order and complexity of stars, flowers, trees, people, society, and, in
particular, the growing order and complexity of your own
mind.

Things run down only if you put them in rational boxes.
If you connect two boxes through a little hole, the gas
molecules in each box will gradually intermingle until the
number of molecules in each box is equal. The two boxes
will have reached equilibrium. This is entropy, a valid scientific idea, but it doesn't run the universe. You can't put
the universe into rational boxes. It is not true that life is

a constant dying. This concept, which finds its root in the Latin expression *"in medio vitae sumus in morte"* ("in the midst of life we are in death"), is not really true. No, we are constantly living, and our living grows ever more complex and more organized, just like life in the rest of the universe.

To be fully alive with all we are and can be, we must let our time-enfolding minds express themselves in our own lives. Becoming aware of this kind of time leads to the possibility of answering that question posed at the beginning of this chapter: Is there such a thing as mind? Is there such a thing as a process of mental becoming which organizes and enfolds all mental experiences through all the living time there has ever been? Let us live with that question for a while and see if the experiences of our own lives contain hints of an answer.

The answer that I discovered emerged from the world in which I lived with Freda. That world differed from the mental reality in which I assumed I lived. For example, when Freda was living in her four-year-old world, she was not conscious of any other time. If I were to live in *her* time, I had to lay aside my minutes and hours and days. I had to learn to live in a time which had already happened, but remained as real mentally as the clock-and-calendar time in my office.

When Freda recovered she convinced me that she could

live in clock time with one mind which existed "now," and, at will, she could live in whole time, with another mind which enfolded all that had ever existed. So Freda finally convinced me that I had two entirely different and separate minds.

All That You Are

This book is the story of my discovery through personal experimentation of the existence of another mind in human beings in addition to our rational conscious mind. This other mind is fully alive to the *wholeness* of time, from the big bang of cosmic origins, through the evolutionary stages by which squiggles of amino acids organized themselves into proto-cells, and on through cellular evolution into complex organisms like plants, animals and, finally, us. For this time-enfolded mind, chronological categories of past-present-future are insignificant.

The rational mind actively uses both sides of our brain and is unbound, free from the self-regulating functions of the body and the living environment. It is unbound from enfolding time and isolated from evolving life.

The other mind—the time-enfolded one which Freda and I discovered—is passively bound to self-regulating body functions (breathing, heartbeat) and to the environment. It uses only the right side of the body's brain, and it enfolds the whole body. It is the mind in which Freda lived in order to fully encompass all that she had been.

It has become apparent that we are in touch with our rational minds about ninety-five percent of our waking time but are only in touch with this bound mind about five percent of the time. I have come to believe that we must fully use both our minds in order to be fully alive.

Personal Research

You will find suggested here experiments which you yourself can do. You will be able to arrive at your own scientific knowledge of this other world in which you unconsciously live, a time-enfolding world rich in sight, sound, taste, smell, and touch. You will be enabled to forge your own scientific tools to explore for yourself this new world. These tools, I have found, need not be computers or calculus computations. What is needed is a basic scientific attitude of openness and fearless devotion to human truth.

This book goes through the stages of my own development of scientific experiments and personal experiences of the other world in which we live. After two chapters of introduction and background, you will be able to experience, rather than just read about, how dreams and spatial environment exist in this other world, rather than in the conscious, rational world. Then you will experience derationalized images and words as distinct from rational images and words. Finally, through experiments with emotion and spirit, your rational mind may discover how to open your life to its full power and potential. Scientific methods of discovery and experiencing will be your tools.

It will take some time to thoroughly assimilate these experiences. Experiments leading to experiences of dreams, space, image, words, and emotions are designed to draw you into a whole knowledge of your true self—all that you are and can be. This whole knowledge must be derationalized, bound to all of life and all of time, not a knowledge censored by the rational, analytical mind. If living fully is wholeness, then scientific knowledge of full human living must be holistic rather than analytical knowledge.

It is only the analytical mind which can open the door to wholeness. This book uses reason, analysis and language to help you discover the whole pattern of your true self, that pattern which cannot exist in the light of reason and language.

An old Zen saying goes, "If you are able to achieve a whole knowledge of a single blade of grass, you will know the universe." Likewise, if you are able to achieve a whole knowledge of your true self, you will know all humankind. Then you will not be alone.

A god can do it. But tell me, how can a man
follow his narrow road through the strings?
A man is split. And where two roads intersect
inside us, no one has built the Singer's Temple.

Rainer Maria Rilke
translated by Robert Bly

II

MIND

Experiencing Another Mind

It's important to check one's feelings about having another mind, a bound-to-body, time-enfolding mind. And it's important to check feelings rather than intellect. The intellect may invent a thousand plausible reasons for denying the other mind, and it may counterfeit feelings as well. So let your true feelings about having two separate minds surface.

We all find it difficult to admit even the possibility of having a whole separate mind independent of our conscious, speaking mind. As a way of experiencing this other mind, try the following experiment. Your rational, linguistic mind will want to keep on reading, but after you have read about this experience, stop; put the book down and try the experiment. Here it is:

> Close your eyes and become aware of a person, a loved one, but do not make any comments about this person to yourself. Let the presence of this person rise up within you. You know "all about" this person, but the all-aboutness is a separate, special kind of knowledge. When this sense becomes clear and definite, then hold it still.

In my first efforts at this experiment I found it hard not to make comments about the person whose presence I was trying to sense and feel. Slowly, I learned to calmly let go of my busy, rational mind. I found myself knowing "all about" this person, though my rational mind remained passive and silent. I couldn't bring my "all-about knowledge" into consciousness, nor could I analyze it.

This was a new kind of mental experience for me. I was

discovering a mind which sensed and felt other persons, but could not speak, think or express its feelings in language. It was a real mind, quite separate from my reasoning one.

Experiencing Rational Mind

Go back to the all-about knowledge of the loved one. Before reading any further, describe the person to yourself in your own words.

略   略

Did you notice a difference between your first "all-about" feeling of the beloved person and your second, linguistic, description of him or her? If the difference isn't detectable, let it go for now and return to the experiment later. You may find that the more often you do the experiment, the more definite and precise your sense of difference becomes. But don't try forcing the experience. Wait until you're ready to try again in a restful, spontaneous way. Don't be misled by your expectations. When I do this experiment, I discover I am reducing the person to parts, to certain characteristic behaviors, colors, clothing, hair, eyes, etc. My rational mind tends to distance itself from the objects I am thinking about. As self-consciousness asserts itself, I become conscious of myself as related to that other person. These are typical behaviors of my self-conscious mind, as it tries to deny that I have an other mind with feelings and sensations of its own.

Keep experimenting with the differences between the feelings that come from your rational mind and those that well up spontaneously from your other mind.

Split Brains, Split Minds

The first chapter contained a very brief account of scientific results that have come from research into the way mind enfolds brain. A major result of such studies has been the growing conviction among scientists that mental intentions initiate the burst of discharges which activate the neuronal events leading to voluntary movements like changing the position of one's finger. This research shows, among other things, that non-material mind—through intentions and decisions—acts upon the material brain. And thus, mind can no longer be dismissed as a chemico-electrical effect produced by brain activity.

I am left with the conviction that humans have not only a mind that acts upon the brain, but two minds which process our experience in quite different ways. Our two minds are not, however, identified with the brain's two hemispheres. Rather, the evolutionary emergence of two hemispheres created the potential for having two minds.

This potential was implicit in the very origins of life. For as soon as the simplest single-celled animal appeared in the course of evolution, a "boundary" was created between it and reality outside it.

This boundary, through billions of years, became ever stronger and more capable of separating the life "inside" from the life "outside." But even though separated, the life "inside" was always bound to the life "outside." In other words, the separating boundary, by its nature, bound inside to outside. In the human species the original potential for having two minds finally becomes realized as this boundary becomes "conscious of itself" through the emergence of our rational minds, which organize the brain's left hemisphere only. This rational mind permits us to step back from that boundary of our experience with the outside to reflect on the mental functioning which ultimately led to this final separation.

The Nobel Prize was given in 1981 to Roger Sperry. By training a biologist, Sperry associated the way people behave with dual mental activity. "Changed concepts of brain and consciousness," he said, "bring a new outlook in which mind supersedes and controls matter." When a Nobel Prize is awarded in science, it means that the scientific community as a whole has accepted the original work of some man. In this case it means that what many today are calling "the mentalist revolution" has been accepted by the scientific community.

The research in chemistry, physics and neurology which

substantiates this mentalist revolution is to be found in an important and exciting new book by Roger Sperry and three other Nobel Laureates. This book, *Nobel Prize Conversations,* is due to appear in the summer of 1985.

Here, I concentrate on personal experiments which you can do yourself in order to experience and live fully with both your minds. In contrast, *Nobel Prize Conversations* discusses these experiences in more theoretical terms that are related to the origins and future of our evolving universe.

To return to Dr. Sperry, the man who pioneered split-brain surgical techniques. Sperry, Bogen, and others experimented with patients after these operations and isolated specific, distinct mental processes which use and organize the split brain's two hemispheres.

Many scientists, including myself, have been doing research in the field of separately functioning right and left hemispheres of the brain. But the important breakthrough for the future of human beings is the "mentalist" revolution. It seems that we have two separate mental organizations—two minds—which process the same signals from our "outside" environment in totally different ways. One mind processes them in a linear sequence; the other mind processes them in self-emergent whole patterns bound to the "outside." These two mental organizations do not reflect each other. Each goes its own way. Each is a different way of being in the world.

Here is Bogen's example of what happens when the brain's two hemispheres are disconnected. Bogen had given each separated hemisphere, each unconscious of the existence of the other, the task of reproducing a cross. The rational mind, which normally uses both hemispheres, was cut off from the passive, holistic data base of the other mind, which uses the right hemisphere. The right hemisphere is united to all the body through its regulation of vital functions like breathing and heart beat. The rational mind, now limited to the left hemisphere and alienated from the rest of the body, used its dominant right hand to draw sequences of parallel lines. The lines expressed length and number but they did not make a cross. The rational mind had analyzed the cross and reduced it to parts, but could not put them together to make the whole pattern of a cross.

The right hemisphere used its left non-dominant hand to draw a cross, but the length of the lines was not equal. It was bound to the *whole pattern* of the cross; it could not see the lines as abstract parts, but it could apprehend the pattern as a whole.

Imagine that your eyes have been fitted with special "Z" lenses which restrict your right eye to seeing only what your left hand does. Now imagine that your right hand, connected only to your brain's left hemisphere, is trying to draw a cross, but the drawing keeps coming out incomplete. There are lines on the paper, but they don't form the whole pattern of a cross.

You throw the pencil down in disgust and say, "This is ridiculous. I know perfectly well how a cross is made. I can show you its parts and how they're put together, but I just can't get my hand coordinated today." Then you are shown another piece of paper with a completed cross on it and are told, "You drew this cross with your left hand."

But you're not conscious of having drawn that cross. If I insist you did, you may protest: "I couldn't possibly have drawn that—I'm not crazy, I know what I've done and what I haven't!" That's the self-conscious rational mind speaking. It has staunch confidence in its ability to know and control, to account logically for its actions.

The importance of these experiments with disconnected hemispheres is not to prove that we have two brains. Their most significant result is what they suggest about the existence of *two* minds rather than one in human beings. When you say, "I didn't draw that," the "I" to whom you are referring is your rational conscious identity. We tend to think our identity is all of us. This identity will go to any lengths to deny that we have another mind. In fact, it may be doing that right now. As you read this book your rational mind may continue to deny that your experiences had anything to do with an "other" mind, a separate mental organization.

Radiant Brain Research

In his long poem sequence "Children of Adam," Walt Whitman wrote

> I sing the body electric,
> The armies of those I love engirth me
> and I engirth them, ...

Whitman's ecstatic celebration of the human body, its wondrous suppleness and intimate beauties, is still as fresh and vigorous as it was when first written more than a century ago. Perhaps Whitman never knew how accurate he was to call the body "electric." For electric it is, and in my own research I regularly use the brain's electric potentials to study the behavior of our two minds in normal activity.

We are, in fact, radiant beings. Over our entire body an aura of electric potential flickers. Around each side of our heads, two halos glow, rather than the solitary one depicted in religious paintings. These two halos exist because each of our brain's two hemispheres generates a different electric potential. The halos flicker at from one cycle per second to over twenty cycles per second.

The halos that encircle our heads are by no means our most powerful auras. Our most potent and beautiful electric potential comes from the center of the chest, the heart. Its frequency is about one cycle per second (sixty per minute), and each cycle radiates through the entire body, including the brain's hemispheres. This is a majestic frequency, strong and steady. It is reminiscent of the dignified pace of a procession,

> All is a procession, [Whitman sang]
> The universe is a procession
> with measured and perfect motion . . . .

Indeed, in medieval and renaissance music, the basic pulse—the *tactus* or "beat"—seems to have flowed along at about sixty beats per minute, a pace perfectly aligned with the movement of a procession and the heart's electrical frequency. No wonder people have long perceived the heart as their center of radiance, their spiritual center.

It is not only the heart and the brain's hemispheres which are radiant; every cell in the body radiates a changing electrical potential. The first cell was an electro-chemical field which balanced what came into it with what went out of it. When this electro-chemical potential ceases, the living cell dies. When our electro-chemical brain waves cease radiating, we are legally dead, according to the statutes of most states.

The brain, heart and intestines radiate electric rhythm in waves. Heart and intestine cells will maintain this rhythmical radiance even when removed from the body. The electric radiance of other cells is not rhythmic but many of your muscles right now are firing at ten cycles per second. With my electrodes I can pick up electric radiance from all over the body. Our true body is a radiant one, and I cannot help thinking of the body as wise, holy, spiritual.

Freda's Mind Experiment

At one point in Freda's discovery of time, which I began to describe in Chapter One, she found herself reclining on a comfortable couch with a white elastic cap pulled down tightly and fastened around her head. Thin wires came from the cap to a wall of electronic equipment. Part of the equipment registered the "halos" around her head. Another part of the equipment was a computer which analyzed and stored measures of those halos (which are, in actuality, flickering electric potentials). Also, there was a very delicate microphone focused on her lips and attached to a tape recorder.

"Close your eyes, Freda," I said. "Wait until your body is comfortable and your mind settles down. Then say anything that comes into your mind. You don't have to speak up; a murmur will do fine."

After awhile, Freda began to speak very softly to herself, "We were going to that dance place with the wagon wheels out in front. Kind of a dive. Kind of smoky inside. . . . low roof. . . . country western band. . . . noisy. . . . those big pitchers of beer on the table. It was long. . . . Oh, I remember, they were all kids from my class at the table. But that was another time. Bill was my date, sitting across from me. I remember, that time we danced a lot.

"He's holding me. . . . I can see my shoes, those brown pumps; there's a smudge on the right one. I can hear the music. . . . violins. . . . sweeping away. My feet hardly touch the floor. It's like glass, glassy. Extends on and on. No one else there but somebody holding me, whirling me. I have a gauzy white dress that swirls out. The night sky is so blue and the clouds. . . ."

There was a pause; then she continued, "I remember, this was a couple of weeks before the accident and I was on the same road." She went on to talk about the accident and her friends. She could do that quite well now.

After the session she said, "I'm doing pretty good now, huh?" "Yes you are, Freda," I said, "So good that I'm going to point out how you were experiencing that past in two different ways. One way you were experiencing time as a rational reconstruction of what had happened. You were remembering things one at a time and making everything fit. Then you saw your shoes."

"Oh, I remember, " she said, "I really saw them; I was really there." "OK, Freda," I said, "hold onto that. I'm going to show you how in the first part you were controlling an idea about the past. You were abstracting time from yourself. Then, when you saw your shoes, you were letting a different mind take over, a mind that enfolds all of time and never is separated from any of what has happened—ever. Forgetting is being separated from part of you which is whole. You have this other separate mind which never did forget anything, couldn't forget anything."

Freda's seeing-the-shoes experience was brief, about sixty seconds. It was the only such experience in a twenty-minute session. If she had been daydreaming and not reporting the experience, Freda would probably not have noticed it. In fact, she didn't really notice the change when she was reporting. She didn't say, "I've just had a mental shift." It wasn't until the research study was over, and she read the transcription of her taped report, that she became aware of the change. Even so, she felt, "Well, so what, I do have a hazy sense of that kind of brief imagistic experience sometimes. It's just my subconscious."

But then she was shown the brain wave recordings

synchronized with her self-report. During the rational linguistic description of the dance, her brain waves were low,
the same in both hemispheres. However, after seeing her
shoes, her brain waves became dramatically different
between the two hemispheres. The computer readout
shows that this was the limit of extreme change in right
hemisphere waves during the session and was also the limit
of extreme change of imagery. Here she could see the
measurement of a mental organization in terms of the limits
of change and its association with a particular physiologi-
cal function. She had seen the measure of her two minds.
When she became able to distinguish these two separate
ways of being in her past, she had consciously discovered
time.

Three Coins on a Table

Conduct the following experiment on yourself. Imagine three coins lying on a table. You didn't have to count
them, you "just knew" there were three. Now imagine four
coins on a table; your knowing them is probably the same
kind of knowing. Now imagine five coins on a table.

Perhaps you still "just know" there are five coins.
However, you may know the five coins because you analyzed them by reducing them into two categories, three

and two. This reduction was the operation of a mind different from the one which "just knew." The "just knowing" is absolute: you either know or you don't. It's a direct revelation, bound to the coins themselves and to their position on the table.

But the knowledge arrived at by reduction is discovery; it is analytical and relative. The rational mind stands back, separates itself from the coins and separates the coins from each other by reducing them to categories.

Perhaps at five coins you still "just knew:" Go on to six or seven. Seven is usually the maximum number which can be absolutely known as direct, bound revelation. Some people have gone to nine coins, which seems to be a limit. Whatever your limit is, you can experience the difference when the unbound rational mind takes over.

❧   ☙

Wechsler uses sets of blocks in his IQ test called Koh's blocks. The subject is given a set of different colored blocks, then shown a picture of a particular arrangement of blocks by color. The time it takes to arrange the blocks to correspond to the picture is an IQ measure. Just as there were two different ways of knowing the number of coins, so there are different ways of arranging the blocks. The subject may "just know" the pattern and arrange the blocks without analysis; or the subject may reduce the pattern to a particular corner and work, through analysis of further reductions, until the blocks are arranged.

If the subject just knew, wouldn't the answer have come revealed absolutely in a flash of insight? There would have been nothing to do; it would just have happened. Can you feel two entirely different mental organizations?

Beyond Freud

Normal conscious mental activity is predominantly rational with occasional, brief, hardly noticed interruptions of a different kind of mental organization. Together we have investigated some examples of these "hardly noticed interruptions," a task which could be described in the words Freud used nearly a century ago:

> The problem was this: to find out something from the patient that the doctor did not know and the patient himself did not know. How could one hope to make such a method succeed?

Freud did very well in creating the myth of humankind driven to the tragic destiny of having to live in two worlds, one conscious, the other unconscious. Now, however, we have techniques to measure brain-waves, as well as means of analyzing the contents of self-reports, that Freud did not have. Today's research can precisely and quantitatively measure what Freud could only deal with subjectively. We can link the passive organization of our other mind to the vivid emotional imagery which is similar to dreams or to the "all-about" knowledge of a loved one.

This mind is holistic, enfolding the right hemisphere and the whole body. However, to link the linguistic self-conscious mind to the left hemisphere is not quite so simple. The linguistic mind needs the right hemisphere as a route to basic spatial images which cannot exist in the conscious mind.

The holistic, time-enfolding mind is immediately bound to body and space; it does not need the left hemisphere in the way the rational mind needs both hemispheres of the brain.

Personal Research

I've been trying to demonstrate the existence and character of this holistic mind by using a minimum number of research experiments done by me and others and a maximum of experiments that you can do yourself. If you have been putting the book down and trying these experiments, you may have begun to experience this other mind for yourself.

Perhaps you're thinking, "But they're not 'real' scientific experiments. I don't have the means to split open people's heads or to measure their brain waves. All I can get are vague inner feelings. That's not scientific." Let me assure you that with all the equipment in the world, results of research into human beings are always vague and ambiguous.

You can do personal research. There are three steps. Suppose I tell you about an experience I've had, and something about that rings a bell, and you become interested. Then, you find you are interested enough to try an experiment to see if that something about my experience is also true for you. Finally, you design your experiment so that you will not be misled by my results.

The method I use to avoid being misled is, first, to push my feelings as far as they will go. When it seems to me that I have experienced a feeling as strongly as I can, I look around for another way to experience the same feeling. Then, once again I push it as far as it will go. Finally, I see if I can detect a difference between these two experiences. Wundt and Fechner, two of the great men who founded psychology, devised a method something like this, only they were looking for the *least* noticeable difference between sensations. In contrast, I am interested in seeing if the differences become stronger and more well-defined as I experiment over and over again with a feeling.

The traditional idea of science is that you can believe what it says about people because scientists have achieved the same results every time they performed experiments. How I wish this would happen! But it never does, not even in sciences like physics and chemistry. In the human sciences, psychology for instance, the method of discovering things about many people and then applying them to one person is particularly difficult. Statistics about many people can never express the unique truth of one living person.

But trying to learn things about one person by studying many people is not the only scientific methodology. Learning things about one person by studying that individual many times can be even more useful. For example, if we learn that one person can run a mile in three and a half minutes, that doesn't tell us how long it takes the average person to run a mile. It simply tells us that it is *possible* for a human being to run a mile in three and a half minutes.

But when we seek knowledge about how *this particular* person thinks, often the only one able to hold the "stop watch" is the person being studied. In many cases *you* are the only person capable of scientifically learning about yourself.

This is the assumption that underlies the experiments in this book. These experiments have ways built into them of checking one result against another result so that in the long run you won't be misled by anyone's expectations of what the results should be. I will tell you openly what *I* expect you to discover in the experiments, but *you* are the one who controls them. Each includes two separate ways of getting the same result. You can check one way against the other.

Human science doesn't promise to eliminate the vague or the ambiguous; it simply offers a way to keep us from being misled by the ambiguity of our experiences. This book suggests experiments designed to help you tell the difference between your two minds. What if, after trying the experiments repeatedly, you find your experience of two minds growing more vivid? What if this leads you to discover even more decisive differences between these two minds? You might justifiably reach the conclusion that you're not being misled by your experiences.

All science proceeds in much the same way. Repeated experiments help refine results and lead researchers to the conviction that they aren't being misled. Elaborate equipment isn't always needed in order for experiments to be scientific or their results valid. Very often, in the history of science, the most astonishing breakthroughs happen when mistakes are made, equipment fails, or totally unexpected results are achieved. Don't be duped into thinking that because you're not conducting these experiments in a roomful of computers and blinking lights, you're not being "scientific." Your basic equipment—two brain-hemispheres and two minds—is a great deal more sophisticated than any state-of-the-art computer.

Science is power. Unfortunately, the scientific power we experience most frequently is the kind that does something to us. We find ourselves being manipulated and controlled by scientific power. What it is doing to us may save our lives. . . . or it may destroy all life.

Personal science, however, gives us the power not to be ruled by those destructive forces which leave us less than we can be.

Observance and Discipline

The existence of that other, bound mind has traditionally been revealed to humans through dreams, prophecy, visions, transcendent experiences, hunches, meditation, the wilderness experience of living at one with nature, myth, archetypal symbol. As T.S. Eliot wrote in "The Dry Salvages,"

> The wild thyme unseen, or the winter lightning
> Or the waterfall, or music. . . .
> . . . . These are only hints and guesses,
> Hints followed by guesses; and the rest
> Is prayer, observance, discipline. . . .

These experiences of the bound mind are mediated by mental imagery, but they always slip through the fingers of the conscious mind, defying analysis and measurement.

However beautiful and important the constructions of rational mind may be, they offer only half a life. Living all the way, living fully as a human being with both minds, requires letting the bound mind claim its own turf. Self-help schemes, regimens of diet and exercise, training in meditation—none of them will benefit us if all our energy is poured into the futile attempt to control all of life by our self-conscious, rational identities. We need to distinguish the separate functions of our two minds, to become comfortable with them.

In the next chapter I will outline those functions and present, for your participation, humankind's long experience with these two minds.

That, while we are thus away, our own wronged flesh
May work undisturbed, restoring
The order we try to destroy, the rhythm
We spoil out of spite: valves close
And open exactly, glands secrete,
Vessels contract and expand
At the right moment, essential fluids
Flow to renew exhausted cells . . . .

W.H. Auden

III

CONSCIOUSNESS

Rational Mind

In the last chapter you experimented with some of the differences between a time-bound, holistic mind and a rational, analytical one. Now I will try to lay out a framework for those differences using rational language. I have come to the belief that the conscious, speaking, rational mind has evolved in human beings *in addition to* the mute, conscious-bound mind which still continues as a separate type of mental organization. *Both minds* make up what it means to be human.

Your rational mind, which thinks it is the only one you have, is unbound, isolated from the body and surroundings. In this isolation it is able to be aware of itself and reflexive; it is what we have come to call "conscious" or conscious-of-itself or conscious of its own functioning. This rational unbound mind is aware of itself in relation to parts and pieces abstracted from themselves and their surroundings. These abstractions, often symbolized by words, are then strung together to form sentences, logical propositions, mathematical formulas. Through these, this rational mind can communicate. It can *say* "I am angry," but it cannot *feel* or express anger. It may analyze the images in a Picasso painting, but it is alienated from the dreamlike source of those images. It guards the gates to the nurturing world of wholeness but it cannot pass through those gates or admit that another mind exists beyond them.

This rational mind, conscious of itself, came to dominate the development of human beings only in historical times. It began to dominate us as a result of the breaking of an evolutionary impasse which kept animals bound wholly and inextricably to their environment. This rational mental organization broke out of its environment and began communicating with itself; it became conscious of itself, reflexive, and able to speak language rather than to emit sounds bound to only one meaning.

In sum, the rational mind exists only because it became unbound, free of both body and environment. It is a magnificent mind, essential if we are to be human. As Albert Camus said,

> We all carry within us our places of exile, our crimes and our ravages. But our task is not to unleash them on the world; it is to fight them in ourselves and others. Rebellion, the secular will not to surrender. . . . is still alive today at the basis of the struggle. Origin of form, source of real life, it keeps us always erect in the savage, formless movement of history.

We can get a sense of how this rational mind evolved, historically, if we consider some dates: Imagine that four billion years ago there was life in the form of proto-cells, squiggles of amino acids floating in the sea.

Then say that three billion years ago there was life in the form of cells, that is, organized electro-chemical bubbles which could separate what was inside from what was outside.

Then, jumping to a billion years ago, let's suppose we find that cells have organized themselves into various kinds of cooperative organisms. And among these we are beginning to see some bilateral organisms; that is, organisms with two sides which are symmetrical to each other but which are mirror images. Fish were the common example of bilateral organization of bodies and brains and they came to rule the seas. They still do.

Now let's makes another big jump to only two million years ago. We find the beginnings of human beings, bilateral cellular organizations with two brain-hemispheres which were beginning to be different from each other. The human minds which organized these hemispheres had begun the process which would lead to that unique leap in evolution, the unbound human mind, conscious of itself yet exisiting alongside the older conscious-bound, human-animal mind.

When did this beginning become fully actualized? Let's say four or five thousand years ago. The Hebrews and the Greeks are good examples. The rational mind became generally dominant in human beings only in historical times. The bound mind is time-bound. It is one with all that has happened in evolution on earth, and one with the arrow of time always changing into the future. The rational mind has imposed on this "whole" time its own linear sequential categories of past-present-future. Notice that past-present-future are linear arrangements of words denoting the grammatical designation of time. The old imperfect tense of "whole" time is an embarrassment in our modern grammars. Modern students who study the classical Latin and Greek languages are often surprised at how often this old "imperfect tense" appears. Their surprise might be lessened if they understood that classical Latin and Greek developed at a time in history when rational mind, finally unbound from its environment, was just beginning to dominate the development of the human species.

Conscious-Bound Mind

This is the mind I've been calling "holistic" or "time-bound." Bound to the body, bound to Freda's kind of time which enfolds all that has ever happened, and bound to its surroundings, this mind lacks reflexive self-awareness. Since it is neither isolated from the body and its environment nor distanced from Freda's "whole" time, it cannot be conscious of itself.

This passively bound mind expresses itself as emotions, feeling tones, dream-like images, revelatory words and numbers. In the evolutionary history of our species, this is our original true mind. Evolving slowly over hundreds of millions of years, it has become a super-animal mind. It won't change or learn in a lifetime. By itself it isn't what makes us human; it is what makes us possible. It passively organizes body functions and passively heals functional imbalances.

"Conscious-bound" is a particular kind of consciousness of which we are usually not aware. All animals are conscious-bound to their bodies, to all that has existed in time, and to surroundings. "Bound" is that all-about feeling of a loved one which I find I can't quite put into words. We experimented with this feeling at the beginning of Chapter Two.

My bound feeling tone is precise and definite. It is an organization of mental communication which I use all the time, but which I can't step back from or speak about. You remember the "all-about" experiment from the last chapter. When I begin to describe a person in language, the precise bound feeling tone disappears. I become conscious of how I put the words together in a linear sequence to make the language. That, of course, is my rational mind taking over.

Think how popular pets have become as people have lost more and more of that bound quality of the healing mind. A dog will sit there with its tongue lolling out, not conscious of its mental functioning; yet pure love will shine out of its eyes. It is bound to love you. Your failures and ineptitudes don't matter at all. A dog is not conscious, in the way a human's rational mind is conscious, of its own functioning. Neither is a dog unconscious. A dog's consciousness is bound to its body and its surroundings in somewhat the same way your holistic mind is conscious-bound to your body and its surroundings. Your bound mind loves your body the way a dog loves. It is bound to that loving.

My holistic bound mind is conscious, but it can't express itself in the linear sequence of sentences, only in whole images and emotional feeling tones, or in words which are wholly bound to a body-emotion or a body-image. The meaning of such words is absolute; they cannot be used linguistically as linear parts and pieces. Often, thoughts which can't be expressed in language are considered to be "unconscious," even though we are aware of a fleeting feeling or inner image. This is communication from your other mind. It is not unconscious; it is conscious-bound.

The Subject was Roses

Some readers may remember seeing the 1968 film "The Subject was Roses," starring Patricia Neal. Miss Neal's performance won an Oscar nomination, and her work was all the more remarkable because she played her role so convincingly shortly after suffering a devastating stroke.

Her story of illness and recovery can help illustrate some of the differences between bound mind and unbound, rational mind.

Medically, a stroke (also called apoplexy) is caused by the rupture or obstruction of a blood vessel in the brain. If this happens in the brain's left hemisphere, paralysis may result on the right side (the left hemisphere controls voluntary movements on the right side of the body because of crossed fibers in the undivided brain stem).

This is what occurred in Miss Neal's case. Immediately after suffering the stroke, she was paralyzed on her right side; her damaged left hemisphere was unable to process mental intentions to move her body or mental acts like thinking, remembering and speaking in sentences. In some ways she resembled Freda, the young girl whose case was described earlier in this book. Like Freda, Patricia Neal seemed to have a body with no mind attached to it.

In fact, however, Miss Neal still had her mind—indeed, her two minds. In spite of a damaged left hemisphere and consequent physical impairment, she was neither insane nor a mere vegetable. For one thing, it became clear almost immediately after she regained consciousness that her holistic, bound mind had kept working all along.

We know, largely from Roger Sperry who was mentioned in Chapter One, that the non-speaking right hemisphere of the brain has a surprisingly well-developed inner world, that it can readily recognize family and relatives and make subtle social distinctions. Patricia Neal's holistic mind recognized her husband Roald Dahl, the short-story writer, and her children Tessa, Theo and Ophelia. She "knew" with this mind, too, that she was pregnant, and the single word "baby" signalled this bound-to-body recognition.

At the earliest stage of her recovery, Pat Neal's rational mind could not yet process these relationships in the linear, linguistic mode characteristic of reflexive thinking. But as her body began healing itself, it became ever clearer that her rational mind was still very much alive. To the consternation of friends who thought he was being cruel, Roald Dahl sent his pregnant wife back to school in a small English village where her teachers were neighbors young and old. She learned again the basics. She learned to walk once more and barely six months after the stroke gave birth to a healthy baby girl.

It wasn't just that Roald Dahl recognized Pat Neal's gritty Knoxville-bred determination. He knew, though he might have lacked all the scientific proofs, that her two minds still existed, even after the horrible devastation of her stroke. While she lay apparently "unconscious" in the hospital, Dahl frequently spoke Pat's name, sensing—accurately—that her holistic mind, conscious-bound and body-bound, would recognize that sound. One could plausibly argue that this bound mind nourished Pat Neal in the journey toward healing, sustained her until her neural equipment was repaired sufficiently to process the intentions and decisions of her rational mind.

Patricia Neal's story is not only a testament to human courage, it is also a revelation of the incredible powers of our two minds. But listening to a story, however inspiring, is a primarily rational activity. In the pages that follow I hope to present you with a few more opportunities to experiment with your awareness of the holistic, conscious-bound mind. This is difficult, sometimes wrenching, work. Be patient with yourself, and don't try to force the "right" results.

You need to recall, first, that the bound mind cannot be separated from the body and its environment. Nor can this mind be controlled by rational thinking. You are healthy when it is healthy; when it's not, you're not. With practice you can become acquainted with this other mind, can keep it in healthy surroundings, can protect it from attack by the rational self-conscious mind.

Mind Experiments

Consider breathing. Your breath is self-regulating twenty-four hours a day. This function of your conscious-bound mind provides precisely the amount of oxygen you need while sleeping or violently exercising. However, breathing is one of the very few intersections of the functions of both your minds. Your rational mind can also consciously control your breathing. That is, you can be conscious of, as well as conscious-bound, to your breathing. Try taking a number of deep fast breaths.

Did you feel a little dizzy? You had too much oxygen in your brain. What if your rational mind had to consciously regulate your breathing day and night to give your body just the right amount of oxygen it needs? Your rational mind, conscious of its own functioning, would probably not do a very good job. What about your liver, your pancreas, your other organs? They continue to inject the precise amount of chemical secretions your body needs to function even though your rational mind, conscious of itself, is not conscious of their functioning.

Perhaps one could say, "Oh, these things are unconsciously controlled." Control? How? Where is the controller? How does the controller work? These glands and muscles communicate with each other and with brain. But brain does not control them. There is no controller. Control is a concept of the linguistic mind. It has no application to the actions of bound mind.

The functions of the conscious-bound mind have evolved through millions of years to do just what they do in cooperation with all of the body. When the body runs short of oxygen, heart and lungs are bound to this stimulus and move to supply the right amount of oxygen. The heart and lungs use precise judgements about how much is needed; they are stimulus-bound and conscious-bound.

Take the balance required for your sense of touch to operate. In some illnesses people's sensory nerves of touch get out of balance and they scream in agony at the mere touch of a sheet. For you to be alive, your holistic mind must be conscious-bound to all of your body and your body's transactions with the touch, light, heat, air, gravity, of your surroundings. Your bound mind keeps you on this knife edge of balance which makes your life possible.

However, by its very nature your rational mind must be *unbound,* distanced and isolated from life. The very act of being conscious is the act of stepping back from the whole flow of life and reducing it to bits and pieces. Having this conscious, speaking, rational mind is a distinctively human quality. By being isolated from living processes, it gives us a feeling of control over life, makes us appear to be masters of the world. But this marvelous mind could not keep you alive for one minute.

Your conscious-bound mind is bound to help your body. It is wholly and absolutely bound to the nurturing, healing functions of your right hemisphere and your whole body. The healing mind is embodied; it uses and is used by the whole body.

Go back to a time when you had left the house, perhaps on a trip, and suddenly you had the feeling that you had forgotten something. Check this feeling out. Is it an "all-about" feeling? Does it have the sense of a whole pattern of living-in-houseness but with something missing from the pattern?

❧   ☙

Because it is a bound pattern you can't bring something missing into consciousness. So you probably try the rational strategy of making a mental list of possibilities: Lights off? Doors locked? Water. . . . oh, I left the water running in the bathroom! This discovery comes from a mind different from the one which was passively aware of an incomplete pattern. The rational mind, conscious of itself, actively attacked the problem by reducing it to parts and sequentially examining them until one was recognized.

The Gates of Eden
Think of Eden, that symbol of wholeness and harmony which is humanity's home. We yearn for that simple immediacy to life, yet we do not find it. The Bible says,

> . . . he placed on the east side of the gar-
> den of Eden cherubim and a flaming sword
> flashing back and forth to guard the way to
> the tree of life. (Genesis 3.24, NIV)

Something was responsible for closing the gates of Eden and that something has guarded them ever more effectively to this day. It is the rational mind, the mind that chose to know good and evil. I don't mean to imply here that it's wicked to be rational or that thinking leads to sin. Remember, the Eden story is not a scientific explanation of our origins, but a potent mythic exploration of behaviors characteristically human. Its insight into who we are shines through on precisely the mythic level.

The Eden story suggests that something about our two-mindedness is both essentially human and essentially perilous. Rational mind wants to guard and lock the gates to Eden, to instill in us an illusion of control. When we capitulate to this illusion, we "sin," to use the Bible's language. Notice, by the way, how many of the stories in Genesis deal with the illusion of control and with its being thwarted by God's higher wisdom (e.g., the tower of Babel, Abraham and Issac, Jacob and Esau, Joseph and his brothers).

It is difficult for us to comprehend how rapidly the

conscious, linguistic mind has come to occupy the almost full attention of our living. Around 1910, Benedetto Croce wrote:

> We no longer believe. . . . like the Greeks, in happiness of life on earth; we no longer believe, like the Christians, in happiness in an other-worldly life; we no longer believe like the optimistic philosophers of the last century, in a happy future for the human race . . . We no longer believe in anything of that, and what we have alone attained is the consciousness of ourselves, and the need to make that consciousness even clearer and more evident.

The damaging thing is not that we humans have rational minds, but that we consistently fall for reason's illusion of control. Basically, that is what happened to Ralph, whose story is told below. He sincerely believed that rational mind could control and cure his whole body. But as I've said, that mind, marvelous though it be, cannot keep anyone alive for a minute. When healing occurs, it happens in spite of the rational mind. Yet that mind jumps up and says, "I did it. I caused it to happen by meditating,

by . . . ." Although the rational mind cannot heal, it says
"I believe in healing." But saying "I believe! I believe!" is
not enough. The trick is to find a way of using your rational mind to discover and open Eden's gates to your
nurturing mind.

Following is a tragic story about a great man who sought
his nurturing mind in the wrong place.

Ralph and Ruth

The orderly was closing the body bag round Ralph's
body. One of the great intellects of our time was dead at
forty-nine. They would wait until the halls were clear to
take him down to the lower level of the hospital.

The old cardiologist looked at me across the bed. He
was one of the best. He still went back to Harvard Medical every year for catch-up courses. His look was bleak.
"My God," I thought, "he still cares after nearly fifty years
of this."

Eighteen months before, Ralph's heart had suddenly
stopped. He had been saved by a passer-by who knew
cardiac pulmonary resuscitation. Ralph had never been
bothered by his heart before. The cardiologist's diagnosis
was ventricular fibrillation, which occurs when the main
pumping function of the heart loses its steady rhythm.
When this happens, sometimes the heart just stops beating. "Beta blockers," drugs usually successful with this kind

of heart problem, hadn't worked. Ralph had gone through all these drugs without results. Neither was there anything surgery could do; the muscle tissues of his heart were healthy.

The cardiologist had suggested Ralph stop smoking and drinking. Ralph had stopped, cold turkey. He had had absolute control of his behavior. Stressful confrontations were ruthlessly excluded from his life. But none of this helped.

Then Ralph heard about research suggesting that meditation can affect ventricular fibrillation. That's when Ralph abandoned medical science and plunged into meditations. He had said, "I appeal to the higher court of reason. I don't want to die—my wife, my work. There is some way, and I believe the power of the human mind can find it."

He had meant his rational mind. He was setting out to cure his heart by the exercise of logic and reason. Some things logic and reason can't do.

Ruth, his wife, had fallen in with her husband's quest for health. He had taken a leave of absence from his university and they moved to California. It had gone pretty much according to form; after meditation there was biofeedback, guided imagery therapy, then yoga.

Finally they came to me. I am not a medical doctor. I am a research psychophysiologist working with the way mind and brain affect each other. They had heard about my brain wave work linking mind and brain. By that time

Ruth's hair had begun to turn white. She was obsessed, ravaged—building a rational nest for her own coming illness.

It is true that brain affects heart, and that my research had shown the association of mind and brain. But Ralph had not been able to distinguish between the mind of reason and the nurturing mind bound to the body. Unlike Freda, who discovered and lived fully in her four-year-old world, Ralph could not let go of his compulsion for rational control of life. He kept trying to subject his body to the strategies of reason.

As I left the hospital room, fingers clutched the sleeve of my laboratory smock. It was Ruth. Her eyes hung back deep in her skull, accusing, "You could have helped."

I put my arms around Ruth and held her. There was nothing to say. Instead, I began a series of experiments which have led to this book.

The Problem with Rational Rules

Our holistic minds are bound to their environment. If we can imagine a sufficiently vivid environment, our embodied bound mind will respond to that environment as though it were really there.

But if we attempt to control or manipulate this environment, our conscious mind will take over and rationally construct an imitation of the environment. The bound mind will not believe this kind of environment for long. Can you believe in what you control? Long human experience says you can't. That's why the biblical stories insist, against all our illusions, that when humans try to trick the conscious-bound mind by playing the control game, they inevitably suffer the consequences.

You may have known someone who last year was being "cured" by guided mental-image therapy. This year they are being "cured" by hypnosis therapy. The "cure" never seems to stop and is never realized. This is not a reflection on the person in therapy or on the therapist. It is an inevitable consequence of trying to use the forces of the bound healing mind in the service of rational conscious identity.

It is not hard to tap into this bound mind. The systems of meditation, biofeedback, guided imagery and yoga to which Ralph devoted his last months do it easily—the first time. Each successive time can be less effective. The experience becomes addictive. In this never-ending circle, people reach for what they know they need, but just as they grasp it, it fades away, slips through their fingers, over and over again. What is happening is that their rational conscious identities are attempting to control and manipulate the bound power of being fully alive.

Our rational conscious identities may become addicted not only to mental exercises but to physical ones as well.

Recent television news programs have reported the growing phenomenon of addiction to exercise by amateur athletes. What begins as an innocent effort to "get the ole bod' in shape" becomes, for some persons, an obsession. Compulsively driven, the athlete's exercise of choice—running, jogging, lifting weights—displaces all other interests and saps the intensity from all human relationships, even the most intimate ones of marriage and family. Thinking to claim control over their bodies and lives, these athletes have lost control, to the point where many of them have sought psychological therapy in an effort to break the power of the addiction.

Once again, I'm not disputing the need we have for both exercise and soundly functioning intellects. But let's be honest. The rational identity can't help trying to take over. After all, it finally achieved dominance over the old super-animal mind after hundreds of thousands of years of struggle. It will use any trick to hide the keys to those gates of Eden. It will obsessively block full living by mimicking it with a set of rules. The same experience happens over and over again as the seeker embarks on yet another new way to fulfill that perceived need for something more than identity.

Do not look for rules. The way to living all the way with all you are and can be is through understanding and accepting another living mind within you. You must absorb some scientific discipline and some spiritual release from identity at the same time. The way is not easy, but the rewards are great. Read on. Remember, it is your rational conscious identity who is reading these words. You should continue to stop reading at the indicated places (◂§ §▸) in order to experience your bound mind. When one's interest in "that other mind" does become aroused, the rational conscious mind may start bullying: "How can you believe that stuff?" There are on the market today many books about healing powers, mind-expansion, altered states of consciousness, helping yourself to health, wholesomeness and thin thighs. Some of this has been satirized recently by Walker Percy in novels like *Love in the Ruins* and *The Last Self-Help Book.*

The problem with much of the material in the self-help genre is that it appeals aggressively to the control techniques of the rational, conscious mind. While it's true that behavior is—and must be—subject to rational control through choice and decision, behavior modification will not, can not, lead to living more fully, to living all the way with all we are. The rational mind's censorship blocks contact with the bound mind's nurturing images and symbols. All the behavior modification in the world won't put us in touch with that other mind where Freda, the young girl whose story was told in Chapter One, discovered the sources of healing and wholeness.

That's why so many people derive such little benefit from programs of diet, exercise and jogging which, theoretically, ought to promote good health and longer life. It isn't that the programs as such are wrong. On a qualified physician's advice, it may, in fact, be excellent for a forty-year-old executive to stop drinking and smoking and start improving his cardio-vascular system by working out. Or it may be fine to spend a relaxed summer at Big Sur, sitting at the feet of a meditation master to learn how mind rules matter. But more often than not, these programs, so innocent and wholesome, wind up feeding the rational mind's hunger for dominance. Their results are frequently ambiguous.

Learning from Children
Watching the human fetus develop from conception, it is difficult not to accept that in some way our fetal development marks a retracing, in the reality of Freda's time, of the still-existing long journey of evolution which led to us. What is more difficult is to fully realize that this evolutionary retracing and enfolding continues after our birth.

Our two brains are the last to complete their evolutionary development. In a new-born the connections between the two brains have hardly begun, and in a young child of two, three, or four years they are far from complete. Thus, a young child in many ways has to cope with the world as Bogen's split-brain patients did.

Notice that the eyes of most young children track reasonably well. Those connections have been made. The sense organs linked to our brain's hemispheres made connection early in our evolution. However, primitive bilateral life forms such as dogfish, which still exist today, had no connections between their brains' hemispheres, so they saw two separate, independent pictures of the world. This is pretty confusing for dogfish, and getting one eye to track with the other is a big evolutionary advantage which we humans had.

One of our eyes always leads; the other eye always follows, and most of the time we don't see double images. Likewise, we have one hand which leads and the other hand which follows. However, little children can do things with one hand about as well as with the other. They are just beginning to develop a leading hand. Those brain connections which permit the left brain to specialize in the fine delicate abilities of the leading hand have not yet been completed.

The brain is still making connections after birth until five to seven years of age. A number of behavioral developments at the five-to-seven-year period indicate that children are activating their rational minds for the first time.

This time is analogous to the historical time of the Hebrews and Greeks when the rational mind finally became
dominant. Recognition of this fact has also influenced the
field of child psychology, especially through the pioneer-
ing work of Jean Piaget, as well as our understanding of
the way moral development occurs in childhood, through
the studies of Lawrence Kohlberg. The pre-seven-year stage
is characterized by confusion and little attention; events
are not in linear sequential context; the flow of time has
not yet become a series of static frames. The child is living through, in its own development, that evolutionary
process of connecting the two bilateral hemispheres. The
old evolutionary mind is still binding child to environment.

Childhood Loss of Bound Mind

Between five and seven years the unbound rational mind
achieves its potential and begins to absorb most of the
child's attention. This was the time when Freud looked
for his Oedipal Complex to develop. Group consciousness and other holistic ways of being result from a mo-
mentary regression to the pre-seven-year-old time when
the human being was bound to and at one with its body.

The Piaget Institute in Geneva has done research on this
period. Annette Karmilov-Smith at Geneva conducted the
following study. She observed two separate groups of

children, one group aged four and five, and the other, seven and eight. She gave each child some rectangular blocks of wood and a straight edge. She then asked the children in each group to balance the blocks on the straight edge. Nearly all the children in each group were able to do this. The question was, how did they do it? Before reading on, close your eyes and see if you can visualize the difference in the ways the two groups accomplished the task.

The younger children would just fool around with the block until they got it balanced. They were living in the world of their bound minds. The older children "got a theory!" They reduced the block to equal parts and predicted it would always balance at the center point. They found that each block, no matter what rectangular shape, could always be easily balanced at the midpoint. The younger children could not do this. To them each new block was a new problem. They could not "abstract," step back and learn about the block; they were bound to the block-in-space.

Now we're going to play a dirty trick on these children. Without their noticing, we will replace these blocks with identical appearing blocks. But these new blocks will have a lead bar hidden in one end. Try to visualize, before reading ahead, how these two groups of children dealt with the task of balancing the trick blocks.

❧   ❧

The older children couldn't do it. They had learned a rational theory, and the theory didn't work. They would try again and again to balance the blocks at the center. When the block didn't balance, they just gave up and said the blocks couldn't be balanced.

On the other hand, the younger children had little more difficulty balancing the trick blocks than the original blocks. The younger child's barely-operating rational mind had not yet learned the theory; but the child's bound mind had been experiencing the block in its own holistic bound-to-the-environment way.

The younger child's hands could feel equal weight on both sides of the cross edge when the block was balanced. In terms of the bound-to-the-block sense of equal weight it didn't matter whether or not the block was placed on the cross edge at the center.

The younger children had no theory to cut them off from awareness of their conscious-bound mind. The older children had become obsessed with the power of this new ability to stand back, to reduce and analyze spatial images and so control their environment. They were unbound and also isolated from the bound mental organization of spatial imagistic communication.

As the seven-to-eight-year-old child develops, his unbound rational mind learns cognitively how to deal with exceptions to his theories and can balance the blocks easily. It is just that at this earlier time the child is overwhelmed with the emerging power of his unbound mind.

Dual minds are species-specific; dual brains are not. All the bilateral animals have two hemispheres in their brains. Dual minds developed only with the human species and this evolutionary development is repeated in infant development. Although the two streams of experience have interacted and become tangled in humans since the completion of the nerve fibers of the Corpus Callosum, connecting the brain's two hemispheres in early childhood, it is now possible to distinguish between the streams and untangle them.

But how difficult it has been for me, and I suspect for all of us, to rationally accept the results of experiments about the existence of this other mind, conscious-bound to the flow of time, to body and to body-surroundings. Keep going; the next chapter shows how dreams are the most practical step in experimenting with the difference between the two minds.

Current-borne, wave-flung, tugged hugely by the whole might of the ocean, the jellyfish drifts in the tidal abyss. The light shines through it, and the dark enters it. Borne, flung, tugged anywhere to anywhere, for in the deep sea there is no compass but nearer and farther, higher and lower, the jellyfish hangs and sways; pulses move slight and quick within it, as the vast diurnal pulses beat in the moondriven sea. Hanging, swaying, pulsing, the most vulnerable and insubstantial creature, it has for its defense the violence and power of the whole ocean, to which it had entrusted its being, its going and its will.

Ursula K. LeGuin

IV

DREAM

Time-Bound

LeGuin uses the jellyfish as a metaphor for dreams. Dreams live in the time-bound world, that world in which *all* times are equally and simultaneously "at home," from the proto-cellular event of four billion years ago, to the time when the jellyfish first began roaming the seas, to the time, only moments ago, when you began reading this chapter. That is why dreams have such power. They belong to no clicking, static frames of clock time—and may thus belong to *any* time of *all* the times of our lives. The phrase "time-bound" may sound restrictive, but in fact it really isn't. Because it is *bound,* a dream touches all times. Perhaps you can remember having dreams in which time seemed to stretch or become jumbled: you were talking to Ronald Reagan when Warren G. Harding pulled up in his car, while spacecrafts from a distant galaxy hovered in the distance! Because they are time-*bound,* dreams put us in touch with the full range of time, remembered and anticipated.

When exposed to the rational mind, conscious of itself, dreams dry out and wither like Le Guin's jellyfish on the beach. Nothing of their power and reality is left. Just as the rational mind tries to enthrall us through the illusion of absolute control over our body functions and surroundings, so too its analytic skills seek to dissect our dreams. Dreaming is an essential part of being fully alive. I find that when I am kept from dreaming, I grow irritable and feel that my being and my living have been diminished. There is, I contend, something about dreaming itself which is crucial for our health and well-being.

In my experiments with myself, I find that my dreaming emerges from that "other" mind, holistic and time-bound, which we began spending more time with in

Chapter Three. I suggest that we take our cue from Wallace Stevens, who wrote in "Sunday Morning,"

> She dreams a little and she feels the dark
> Encroachment. . . .
> As a calm darkens among water lights

Dreams are the dark speech of the spirit. How do we hear them speaking? Here are some ways.

History of Dreaming

Let's begin by feeding some facts to the rational mind. Dreams have been used to reach the spirit since the dawn of history. Some of the most renowned Greek oracles used dreams as spiritual power to effect healing and security in the world. At the oracle of Delphi there was always a long waiting list for appointments. The writers of the Bible, in both testaments, assumed that dreaming was God's most common means of revealing his will and plan to human beings. Joseph, one of Israel's patriarchs, gained both reputation and power as an interpreter of dreams at the Egyptian royal court. David, ever Israel's example of virtuous kingship, was warned to forget about building God a temple after God had instructed the prophet Nathan in a dream. A later Joseph, Mary's husband, was comforted in a dream after he had discovered his betrothed wife's pregnancy.

Even when they "interpreted" them—a rational, analytic activity—the ancient peoples were inclined to regard the power of dreams as sacred and thus as self-legitimating. The important issue was not so much the interpretation given to dreams but the dramatic revelation of divine power through the interpreter. The dream was the thing, because there the numinous power pulsed.

Even after the conviction that dreams are divinely revelatory began to wane, they were often still respected—sometimes feared—as significant human events. Shakespeare's Hamlet voiced what many, then and now, dread:

> To sleep: perchance to dream: ay, there's the
> rub;
> For in that sleep of death what dreams may come
> when we have shuffled off this mortal coil,
> Must give us pause. . . .

Dreaming is feared—if not because it tells us what God wants, then because it signals the presence of that time-bound mind which we don't want to believe we have.

Dreams have, of course, always had their detractors, their despoilers. But not until quite recently did dreams become the object of systematic measurement and research by scientists. Some of Sigmund Freud's earliest papers on psychoanalytic subjects were devoted to the significance of dreams as sources for examining the contents of what he called the unconscious. Carl Gustav Jung broadened the base of dream research by proposing that dreaming is not limited in importance to the personal unconscious of individuals but is shaped as well by the innate mental structures—archetypes—that originate in the collective unconscious of our species.

So we live in an age when dreams have once again recovered a certain stature. This next section will provide some further information about dreaming and will provide some opportunities to experiment with my contention that dreams arise from the holistic, time-bound mind.

Body Dreaming

Rapid eye movements during sleep (Stage REM dreaming) are connected with the whole body through the brain's right hemisphere. Stage REM dreaming is an imagistic mental stream different in kind from the linguistic rational stream of waking experience. In Stage REM dreams there seems to be little activity in that bundle of nerves which connects the brain's hemispheres. This leaves no effective way for the rational mind to use the holistic imagery that the bound mind is dreaming. This is another way of saying we become "unconscious" when we sleep.

This vivid dreaming in the first part of REM sleep is not just the right hemisphere dreaming; it is the whole body dreaming. Have you ever seen a dog's legs twitching while dreaming? Human beings' legs often do too. Both our legs and his legs are involved in a REM dream. We and the dog are both paralyzed when we have this kind of dream. The body is so completely involved in this dream that we could seriously injure ourselves if we were not paralyzed. We just twitch slightly.

Dreams are bound to our whole body the way our other mind is bound. Have you had the experience of a body sensation activating a vivid mental recall of a past experience? The body sensation could be a blow or a sudden shock to a body muscle. It could be a sudden sensation of heat or cold. It could be a caress. The experience lives in one's body. The whole body is part of and participates in the life and dreams of your body-bound mind.

Becoming aware of dreams is one of the ways to learn to be aware of the time-bound, body-bound mind. Vivid dreams occur about every ninety minutes; it is difficult to be aware of them. Think of a time when you were telling a just-experienced dream. Didn't the actuality of the dream begin to run through your fingers and fade when you tried to put it into words? Wasn't your telling of the dream a narrative story that really wasn't like the atmosphere of the dream at all? The trick is to find ways of being aware of dreams that do not let the rational mind take over. It will if it can. You will be convinced that you know your dream when you actually don't.

Recording Dreams

Here is a formal way of experimenting to become more aware of the body-bound mind in dreams and throughout the whole day.

I find a daily record useful. Just before going to sleep, I briefly record the day's events, paying attention to flashes of imagery, hunches and feeling tones. They are the way the bound mind communicates. This should take a minute or two; then I place the pad of paper and the pencil on the bed next to me. I have found an 8-1/2 x 11 pad is most convenient; I fasten the pencil to the pad so it won't be lost during the night. As I go to sleep, I make sure the location of the pad and pencil is in my mind. I don't concern myself with whether or not I will dream or with how well I will sleep. My only concern is the location of the pad and pencil.

There are times during the night when I turn over or when I almost wake up. Ordinarily one doesn't pay attention to these episodes and has forgotten them in the morning. Now, however, I have acquired the habit of reaching for paper and pencil when they occur. It isn't necessary to turn on the light, to open my eyes, or even to wake up. I can feel where to write on the paper. I write a few nouns or a drawing that is descriptive of the dreamscape, the dream surroundings. I don't write sentences or try to think about or try to understand the "meaning" of what I have written. That would allow my rational mind to take over. If it does, the dream will dry up and wither like LeGuin's jellyfish.

In the morning I try to decipher the words or drawings. I still don't try to understand the "meanings." I just accept them as they are and go on about the morning's activities. The time involved to do this is negligible. It may be I will put nothing down, or that what I have down is not decipherable. That is not important. What is important is just establishing the routine. No one can make this kind of thing happen. The routine will eventually let it happen. Then meanings rich with emotional feeling tones and the whole, vivid images living in the bound world will appear.

The actual dream is not available to our rational minds. We can't record the dream rationally. Try recording, for example, any emotion, asleep or awake. It slips through your fingers. You can write around it or about it, but the actual experience of the emotion isn't available. This is also true with dreams. Dreams are made of emotional feeling tones which can't be put into words. But the dreamscapes, the landscapes of the dreams, can be recorded with little contamination by your rational mind. These "dreamscapes" are the images, the emotional feeling tones, and the body sensations of the dream—what it feels like to be there. They are even more precise with meaning than a story about the dream would be.

And your "dreamscapes" are also "scapes" of time. I'm sure you've had dream experiences similar to the ones mentioned at the beginning of this chapter, where environments of years ago appear with what happened yesterday. Your dreaming mind is never shocked as your rational mind would be. Your dreams are bound to the reality of whole time—all that has ever happened—rather than the linear, moving-picture frames of static clock time. The flow of movement in a movie is an illusion. The time of dreams is reality. Your dreams of floating, sinking, flying may enfold the real, exisiting time of the first cell.

The dreamscapes will be a key to the feeling tones of the dream. Do not try to record more than the "scape," the environment of the dream. When you try to record the dream as a story (which it isn't), you are using your rational mind. It will take over and counterfeit the actual experience.

As you have sleeping dreams, so do you have waking dreams. These are those everyday hunches, hardly noticed images, and feelings. Record them too.

What follows is a sample experimental record which

started with "dreamscapes." It was made by a burly, sloppily dressed man, "Tom," who was a sales manager of a corporation with offices atop one of those downtown towers that dominate urban skylines. Reluctantly he had agreed to be a subject in a brain wave research project I was running. He is still burly and bushy, and any suit he puts on becomes instantly rumpled. Also he has become executive vice-president of his corporation. His is an example of how your record might look. I have put examples of his record at the end of chapters throughout the book, but don't try to imitate the examples. If you do, you will make a rational structure of your own record. The pattern of your dreamscape must be unique to you. Notice that in this example, experiences of the time-and-body-bound mind are recorded as they occur. There seems to be little distinction between sleeping and waking.

For this experiment to work it must become a part of your daily living. Take your time. The precise emotional feeling tones of mental experiences must be identified and assimilated. To experiment with whether or not you can discover two minds within your one self, and can tell the difference between them is a *process*. Gradually this experimental design will develop toward the final resolution of the book.

Tom's Dreamscape Record
September 12th

Morning first day. Had no dreams last night. Told him didn't dream. Here I am a guinea pig—once a week for ten weeks. Must have been crazy. Normal day's routine except Peter stabbed me in the back at the meeting. Big friend!

At the hall corner to restroom. Flash of image, blue dress, white hair, glint from glasses—Mother—white fuzzy sense of space—no emotion—stayed with the image and found constriction in chest.

Driving home. Chest constriction back. Tried staying with it. Nothing happened.

Got on John's case about cleaning plate at dinner. Damn! Kept replying to Peter over and over in my mind—TV show but my replies to Peter back more when show over.

Dream—black silhouette of Mother in wheel chair—stayed. No surroundings. But

space—some kind of spatial slot. Mother
getting closer without getting bigger. Woke
up frightened. Chest, throat, muscles tense.
Heart and breath fast.

The Kind Gates of the Body

Why should anyone, especially a busy businessman like
Tom, go through all this record keeping just to find
wholeness? Dreams aren't the bound mind; but dreamscapes are the road to that world of space, shape, form
and emotion which is the nurturing, conscious-bound mind.
The formal experience of dreamscapes prepared him for
his discovery of the bound mind in what followed. The
experimental record is far more than dreams. It will record how intimacy with holistic mind grows just through
the experience of taking care of it.

Think about dreams the way W.H. Auden does:

Simultaneously, as soundlessly,
Spontaneously, suddenly
As, at the vaunt of the dawn, the kind
Gates of the body fly open
To its world beyond, the gates of the mind,
The horn gate and the ivory gate.

There are a few more things to know about dreams before one starts experimenting. First, my experience is that both minds share the same experiences, but they are aware of those experiences in different ways. In that sense they live in different worlds with the same experiences.

The bound mind, using the brain's right hemisphere and the body, is the dreamer. The dreamscape is the world of the bound mind, not of the rational mind. Perhaps, as I suggested earlier, you have had the experience of dreams which seemed to be enfolded in time. Persons whom you knew many years ago are just as fresh and immediate as people you met at lunch yesterday. This is an example, through a dream-experience, of the time which Freda discovered when she and I began living in her four-year-old world, as I related at the begining of Chapter One.

A dream cannot be conscious of itself. Your dreamscape does not tell you anything about the way your rational mind operates but it uses the experiences of the rational mind. We are conditioned in our culture to believe that dreams tell us secrets about our "conscious" life. They do, but not secrets about how our mind, conscious of its own functioning, works. The hardest temptation to resist in recording dreamscapes is to treat them linguistically, as stories. Nor are we recording messages from our conscious-bound healing mind to our rational mind, conscious of itself. Each of our two minds lives in a world of its own. Our dreams express the experiences of the rational mind, but only as those experiences are perceived by the mind bound wholly to the body, to its environment and to the arrow of time.

A good therapist can put dream experiences to use, but there is no therapeutic or psychological purpose in keeping this experimental record. Its purpose here is simply to record a growing intimacy with wholeness and the nurturing time-bound mind.

Dream Experiences

This is not to say that dreams are not practical. Sometimes a dream of a burglar in the house reveals that there really is a burglar in the house. The holistic mind is passively bound to the whole pattern of our experience. Let's say you came home late. Your holistic mind may have noticed a closet door slightly ajar which you had left closed. Your rational mind, conscious of itself, didn't notice. It's only aware of one thing at a time in a linear sequence; it can't be aware of whole patterns. So you go to sleep with an incomplete pattern in your holistic mind. You immediately dream of the burglar, which satisfies the incomplete pattern. You wake up, call the police and the burglar is apprehended! Trust your dreams; they are absolute in their own world.

Don't be afraid of dreaming bad dreams. Nothing in them can hurt you; they don't necessarily mean there is anything wrong in your life. Your conscious-bound mind is the one bound to time and evolution. It has been afraid of your getting eaten by monsters or of falling into a pit for hundreds of millions of years. The fact that you exist to be dreaming is evidence that your holistic mind has been successful in helping your ancestors survive.

Say you dream you are being chased by a tiger. You are running in panic. Remember, this tiger can't hurt you. There's nothing wrong with running or the emotion of fear that goes with it. That is your evolutionary way of survival. However, you don't have to run in your dream. You might stop; you might kick the tiger in the nose; the tiger might chew on your foot for a while; it might go away. Whatever happens can't hurt you. Once your dreaming self has become convinced that it can't be hurt, you may find the dream experience of fear and running to be a healing one. These periodic spasms of emotion and imagery through the day and night are ways your holistic mind keeps its patterns of experience whole.

A word of warning: If you follow this discipline of dreamscape recording, you will become more aware of and intimate with your dreams. There may be times when you feel you can control the dream. Don't do it. It's a way your rational mind can get in and counterfeit your true dream experience. You will wind up with nothing more than identity-serving daydreams while you sleep. There is overwhelming pressure from your rational mind to make sense of these experiences outside its control, to keep the gates to Eden locked.

One subject I knew became so adept at rationally controlling her dreams that she was able to have vivid dream affairs with fascinating men who were not her husband. Even her physical body had orgasms. She was fooling her bound mind which took her rationally controlled environment to be real. Soon the dreams became only self-serving. Her marriage broke up. She had lost the way to the human integrity and wholeness offered by the bound mind. Remember, bound mind has its own way of getting even if you try to trick it!

Your personal identity is constructed by your rational mind, conscious of itself. To exist, your identity has to maintain a consistent image of itself. This is a fragile, relative kind of existence. Your rational mind must be aggressively busy with this construction of an identity. Your rational mind does dream to some extent, but these rational dreams are without emotion or vivid images and often consist of repetitive rounds of words. These words are "tapes" intended to bolster self-identity; e.g., "I'm never sad or hurt; big boys don't cry," or "I'm a genius—can I help it if these clods don't understand that?" Don't record those tapes in your dreamscape record.

Distinct from your identity is the world of living all the way with all you've got, with the whole pattern of your experience. It is passive; its consciousness is bound to body, time and surroundings; it cannot isolate and control itself. It is absolute, immediate, and spontaneously self-emergent. It is nurturing, comforting. As you work through the book the dreamscape record will become the foundation for routines with surroundings, images, words, emotions and spirit. In the next chapter, you will be introduced to the "scape," to bound mental space. But first try having a waking dream about primal space.

The Primal Sea Experiment

Close your eyes, take five breaths. Let all time enfold you; there is no past-present-future. Now imagine yourself a single cell. There are no eyes or ears; everything is dark. There is nothing but skin, no arms or legs, no nerves to the skin, nothing but a difference in electrical potential between what is inside and what is outside. Let this feeling of electric differential flood your entire being with knowledge of the difference between what is outside and what is inside.

Stay there in the primal ocean and make one more shift back to a time when you (as the cell) didn't even have a skin. There is no electric differential; let go; nothing but darkness. You are nothing but a proto-cell, a floating squiggle of amino acid molecules. How is any kind of mental existence possible here? Wait. Feel yourself; there is a differential. There is up and down, weight. This differential is not external to you; it is internal. It is the basic knowing of the universe, gravity. Gravity is the first stuff of the bound mind. Aren't your earliest dreams of falling, flying, sinking? We considered these in the previous section of this chapter. These dreamscapes are of up-down gravity.

Imagine space as an infinite bed sheet; but the sheet has depressions, which are rates of change in the fabric of space. Anything near a depression tends to roll into it. This is not a force like electricity, but a property of universal space itself. It is immaterial; science cannot measure it. From a material, measureable point of view gravity doesn't exist; yet it is the strongest force in the universe. It can be thought of as a mental expression of all that is, of life, and of the bound mind. It is not only space; it is also dreamscape, the original reality of the unbound mind.

Still being this squiggle of amino acids, feel, inside you, the knowledge of the universal dreamscape. Even in this "primal sea" there is a "knowing" that belongs to gravity—and there is a "bound universal mind" that knows. But it is the *bound* mind, not the rational mind of words and logic.

The research question here is: what are the differences and similarities we can detect in ourselves between the way gravity organizes space and the way mind has evolved to organize cell, body and brain?

Stable Space

The first mental act of the first living proto-cell must thus have been the inner "knowing" of gravity. Gravity is the only sensory event which occurs inside an organism. Nothing is occurring outside the organism when gravity is sensed. It is an internal event. It is immaterial, without substance.

Where is the force when Newton's apple falls? It is in the apple, the weight of the apple. The sense of up-down inside an organism is always present. It is the first sensation of life, and it is embodied in the organism. It is stable, and this stability is the first necessary step in the development of the original bound mind.

The second step was the development of the cell's physio-electric membrane, a difference in electro-chemical potential which keeps some ions in and others out. This is the first "outer" sense, akin to touch, for the cell's membrane is, in effect, its "skin." Now life has developed the sense of inner and outer, of extension and distance. But this sense is also immaterial, like the gravitational knowing at the origins of the unbound mind. The senses of hearing, seeing and smelling can be thought of as windows developing in the cellular membrane. And thus, the beginnings of life had the stable, ever-present, inner-spatial images of up-down and inside-outside.

The third step was the development, in the phylum which led to fish and human beings, of bilateral cellular reproduction. Hold your hands together as though praying; then let your hands swing apart. Your hands, pressed together, are bilateral mirror images of each other. The inner bound mental creation of space has now acquired direction, right and left.

These three mental images are the framework of the bound mind. They are abstracted in the three Cartesian dimensions of space: up-down, side-to-side and out-from. Development of our bound mind depended on the stability of these inner mental images of space. These dimensions are purely the bound mental organization of space. Matter is merely a "warping" of that space.

The world of primal space is thus the mental imaginal organization of the dreaming mind. This is why paying attention to the "dreamscape" instead of the dream narrative is so important. A rational narrative hides that whole time which enfolds all the life that has ever been. Through the dreamscape we live fully with all life.

Provided our rational minds do not counterfeit them, our dreams are basic tools that equip us to discover that other mind, bound to all time, to space and to the first evolutionary stirrings of life in our universe. As you gain

experience in keeping the experimental dreamscape record, you will also learn to trust your dreams. When that
happens, you will be on the way to discovering how to
become fully alive, how to live in harmony with all time
and all life that exists—or ever has existed. The next
chapter will suggest some experiments through which you
can expand your potential for living fully still further by
aligning yourself with space.

Leonardo da Vinci's reveries, like those of most children, also turned to the human body, and to the earth, its mountains and rivers and its shattering cataclysms. Here again, Leonardo's way was to take these reveries seriously and follow them to their consequences: anatomy and geology. . . . Each time Leonardo started working on anatomical studies his mind was likely to turn to problems related to the structure of the earth. Here one can sense an identification in fantasy of the big body of earth and the lesser body of a human.

Gibson

V

SPACE

A Hunter in Harmony with Space

George, wide-shouldered, athletic, was a subject in an investigation of perceptual integration with space. He became very good at it. The result was, of all things, that he became a bow hunter. The killing of innocent animals does not sound like an ecological harmony with the spiritual world. But with George it was exactly that. He learned so well to be in harmony with space that he could literally immerse himself into his natural hunting environment. He let himself become one with the earth, the trees, all the living things around him. In other words, he learned how to allow his body-and-time-bound mind to occupy all his attention.

Watching George crouched immobile and passive by the trail, one might think him lacking self-conscious awareness. That would be right. He was enfolded in evolving time. He might also appear to be lacking volition, but this would not be true. When his prey appears, he flashes into instant and effective action to consummate a focused intention. His very passive embodiment in his environment allows the fullest expression of volition and intention within that environment. Intention may falter when a sequence of rules from the rational mind intrudes. But when intention is bound to environment-time, it cannot change unless the environment changes.

Once he kills his prey, a shift occurs. George finds his rational self-conscious mind occupying his attention again. Unbound from body and surroundings, he sees himself consciously as a great hunter. He begins to justify his acts in words which imply that his hunt and kill were cognitive and reasonable actions. He describes his intention to kill in rational, consistent language. But now, since his experience in the space project, he also knows which is his rational mind, and which is the healing mind bound fully to his environment. He has learned to intentionally use both minds.

The rational mind only comprehends intention in terms of sequential steps in a rational system, and indeed intention may be very effectively carried out in this manner. But from where did volition come? While George's rational mind undoubtedly acted to plan the hunt, the actual hunt existed in the world of his bound mind, and that is where the pure intention to kill existed.

Imagine the wholeness of George being at one with his surroundings, letting his nurturing, conscious-bound mind occupy his awareness, and then imagine how the sensation of wholeness disappeared when he got caught up in the rational problem of how to present his identity as a hunter.

When George is asked, "Do you feel better, deep down, going fishing or going to a social function?," his rational mind, conscious of itself, takes over and constructs his rational identity replete with shoulds, oughts and rules. He can feel his breathing tighten up just thinking about it. It's not good for his health, but it's the price he pays for being human. This price we all gladly pay; it has made us masters of our world; it will enable us to seed the stars.

While we may be willing to suffer illness for human destiny, let's not suffer it unnecessarily. We have the means to fulfill our rational, conscious human identity and, at the same time, to keep our spirit of oneness with this universe we are out to conquer. We can have both.

George and I became friends. I had shot bows since I made my first one when I was eleven years old. I wasn't a hunter, as George was, but I was close enough to him to experience a hunt in a separate world of space and time. George knew this world because he could live in it with a bound kind of awareness whenever he chose to switch from his unbound linguistic world.

Yet here I was superbly trained in the theory and research of perception. I was the scientist; yet I couldn't experience the reality of my research. I studied George carefully when we went on camping trips, and gradually I became aware of a change in the way he aligned his body with gravitational space when he switched into his hunting kind of awareness.

I also became aware that George was slipping into Freda's kind of time. All time was present and real to him. He was one with the squiggle of amino acids we have imagined. He was one with all the evolving time of the forest. Aligned with space, George had the aura of having been there by the trail forever.

Standing in Harmony with Space

Try this simple muscle relationship with space. Stand up; tighten the muscles in your lower back and buttocks.

This will tuck your buttocks in. Leave the sphincter muscles of your rectum relaxed. Let your knees bend slightly. Now using the sheath of holding muscles around your abdomen, pull your skin and navel upwards. Do not use the active muscles which pull your stomach in; leave them relaxed. Now let your shoulders slump. If you dropped a plumb line from your head, it would pass through your shoulder joints, your hip sockets and your ankle joints. The center of gravity is where your pulled up navel is.

It may take a little while to accomplish this; those particular muscles are hard to isolate. You are using them just to get your body in harmony with gravitational space. These are not rules for how to stand, just ways of being aware of the feeling of the body in harmony with space. Try walking. You will find yourself taking smaller steps lifting your knees slightly.

❧ ☙

Doesn't this kind of walking feel free and effortless? Once you have the feeling, forget about the muscles. That will take time, but be passive. Let the emotional feeling tone become a part of you and your awareness of your body in space.

When I started following these directions, it took me several months of disciplined standing and walking before I could record that free, effortless feeling that for me is always on the edge of jogging. I felt an unspeakable feeling of rightness when I stood and walked. Also, I never felt that click-in of rightness when I walked in any other way. I began to believe that I was not kidding myself, that I was not being misled by my expectations of these experiences.

However, I could not assert the validity of my personal experiment because it was a reduced and very limited part of me and all my possible experiences. I still could not perceive, with any of my senses, this world which George could live in with all his senses. He could see, hear, smell, feel with his skin, his muscles and his sense of balance, this separate world.

I knew that all our senses use the same perceptual code; they all perceive in the same way. So I determined to start with one sense as a way to getting to all of them. I had begun to realize that this other bound world was whole; it would require living fully in time with everything I had to experience it.

The key to this problem was found in some work I had done on a perceptual phenomenon called "blind sight." Here is a research example:

There are primitive mental processes which have transmitted sight since early evolution. An example is seeing something "out of the corner of our eye" without knowing what it is. Some people become blind because of damage to that part of the brain which receives electro-chemical impulses from the eyes. They say, "I am blind. I can't see anything." But they can accurately point to a light source while their rational mind is saying it can't see a thing. Here is a blind man, for example, whom we'll call Albert. He is distinguishing a circle from an X while saying, "I can't see anything, but I have this feeling that the X is on the right. But I just can't put it into words."

He was able to see enough "out of the corners of his eyes" to communicate it emotionally. This same information was transmitted to the rational linguistic mind which was completely unable to process it. The speaking mind was blind to that information. The holistic mind, conscious-bound to body and surroundings, could perceive a whole primitive image but could not speak of it. This whole primitive image extended from the early evolutionary time when cellular bound mind sensed up-down and out-from, which was the beginning of sight. This image could not be broken down into the linear sequential processes of the rational mind which lives in clicking clock time.

Holistic mind is bound to the mental organization of this sub-visual system of "blind sight." But the unbound rational mind, conscious of itself, cannot be aware of what you have seen. This phenomenon of blind sight is also well-known to pianists and other keyboard artists. Concert-goers are sometimes startled to see a pianist gazing "into space" while playing a fiendishly difficult passage that seems to demand close open-eyed attention to the precise position and movement of the hands. The pianist could also play the piece with his eyes closed; after all the playing at the technical level is nothing more than a well-rehearsed muscle pattern. However, one can conceive that the artist stares "into space" to bring the whole of all of his senses into the creative act. If he looked directly at his hands he would be in danger of his rational mind taking over.

Do these artists "see" their hands? No, if by seeing one means a conscious awareness by the unbound, rational mind. But that primitive visual system linked with the bound mind does see, and sees very precisely the intricate patterns involved in every measure of a Mozart concerto or a Bach "Trio Sonata."

Perhaps more than any others who have inhabited this place we call "America," the Native American Indian peoples were astonishingly skilled at combining the sense of destiny, of mastery over environment, with the sense of absolute harmony with their physical surroundings. Perhaps it is because they were so completely in touch with holistic, body-bound mind, as in this Papago Indian "Dream Song,"

> Where the mountain crosses,
> On the top of the mountain,

I do not myself know where.
I wandered where my mind and my heart
seemed to be lost.
I wandered away. . . .

Walking in Harmony with Space

Since this primitive system of perception we are calling "blind sight" was non-verbal and conscious-bound to its surroundings, I concluded it was a function of the other mind which I had disentangled from the rational mind in my brain wave experiments. It was the world of the bound mind I was seeking. Here is the experiment I finally worked out.

Go out for a walk around the block while keeping your body relationship with gravitational space which you had when standing and walking before. Keep your navel pulled up, buttocks relaxed and tucked in, knees bent. Become aware of the fingers of your right hand swinging to line up with your left toe as you step forward; then of your left fingers lining up with your right toe. Keep this up until the rhythm becomes a part of your body and your surrounding body space. You may feel your shoulders swinging slightly to the rhythm, your whole body settling into a rhythmic relation to its surroundings. Don't try to make it happen, let it happen. If it doesn't happen the first time, or the fifth, that's fine. Try another day until it does.

Your eyes are still aware of your swinging fingers. Now slowly raise your head while continuing to look at your fingers; then slowly raise your eyes until you can no longer consciously see your hands, but you "just know" when they are swinging up and back. You are actually, physically, still seeing your hands even though you think you are not. Remember, your eyes have this primitive visual system called blind sight.

Now comes the crucial revelatory moment; as your eyes move up, your continuing blind awareness of your fingers swinging can short-circuit your rational mind, and you will find yourself seeing a brief flash of the conscious-bound world of your body-bound mind.

This seeing is conscious-bound to the whole pattern of surrounding space. You are conscious-bound to your surroundings. You have been separated from time and environment by your rational mind, self-conscious of its own functioning. There is no longer a distinction between you and your surroundings. You are your surroundings, and they are you. It is a different world. You are touched by immortality and connected to the whole life of your planet. There may be a floating sensation; your surroundings may have a fluid aspect. On the other hand, you may not be able to put your finger on any one sensation. You may just feel a background of harmony with yourself and your surroundings. There is no particular way you are supposed to feel, but in any case don't let yourself become rationally self-conscious of the feeling. Whatever you feel, stay with it. Give yourself to the experience. Go all the way. Try it.

But don't be misled by expectations. This is your experiment. Push your feelings to the limit and then compare them to the feelings of normal walking. Each time compare the differences in your feeling of walking through the time-bound, body-bound, surroundings-bound "scape" of your holistic mind and the world you experience with your rational mind. See if the differences increase as you continue the walking experiments.

Once you have the clear emotional feeling tone of this walking, forget about the way in which you arrived at the feeling. Let it happen to you as it will. It is the revelation of the feeling tone which is important, not the way you get there. As usual, your rational mind will want to take over; if it does, you will lose the feeling tone. However, once you have the feeling tone you can do the same thing jogging as well as walking. You can jog in harmony with the whole web of life and time of your planet.

In my original experiments, this astonishing feeling occurred only in flashes. After several years I am still doing this experiment. I love those tantalizing flashes of a world that is whole, beautiful, enfolded in time and at peace with all the life that lives and has ever lived on this planet, what we have come to call in scientific jargon "the biosphere."

I still only get flashes. If I experienced extended periods of being in that world, I would strongly suspect that my rational mind had taken over and constructed an illusion of wholeness. Flashes of whole images are comforting to me because they are difficult for the rational mind to construct in its linear sequential way.

I'm sure I will never be able to live in that whole world. After all, I am just a rationally trained scientist. However, over the years my recorded results have been consistent and compel me to believe that I can, to an extent, tell the difference between the two separate minds which are me and the two worlds of those minds.

This walking or jogging is a special way of being in the world. If you discover, through your own experiments, that you are letting an awareness of your surroundings which is time-bound and body-bound flow through your life, try to lengthen it in natural surroundings. Surrender the clock ticking control strategies of your rational mind. Make these experiments a part of your daily life. Live in harmony with space and you will begin living in harmony with your body. This harmony is the foundation of healing, of feeling good and living a long time. It is grace in space.

If you have thoroughly experienced this emotional feeling tone, you will know it absolutely and precisely. It will be like turning on a switch when your mind, body and surroundings are in harmony. You will find yourself naturally gravitating to healing surroundings and will know when you are in a destructive place. We often have these feelings naturally and call them "hunches" or intuitions. Or they may be imagistic flashes which disturb your rational mind and are hardly noticed. Normally these kinds of feelings occur only about five percent of the time and are not acted upon, do not become effective in your living. Now this emotional feeling tone can be experimented with and its effectiveness tested in your daily life.

As a side benefit of experimenting with "grace in space," you will become aware of that sheath of holding muscles around your abdomen which you activated when you pulled up your navel while standing. As you maintain this alignment with gravity while walking or jogging, your stomach will begin to become flat naturally, without sitting-up exercises.

But remember that these experiences of harmony with space will not develop fully and will not last unless, in parallel, your rational mind comes to an understanding of how the gates to Eden came to be opened. The next few sections of this chapter are directed at an understanding by your rational mind. Don't skip them to get on to more holistic experiences. These sections are indispensable to the processes beginning to take place within you.

Holistic Ecology

A great deal is said or written these days about ecology and the pollution of life on earth. But this saying and writing abstracts into parts what can only exist whole. Ecology doesn't stop with your skin. There is also the ecology of your mind which is bound to time and body. If you can achieve the bound-to-space walking or jogging just described, you will have experienced holistic ecology.

Holistic mind is an ecology of body senses, all time and body space. It knows absolutely and with immediacy that it must have holistic surroundings. Being fully alive depends on our gravitating to harmony with our surroundings. If our holistic mind is inextricably bound to body embedded-in-space, then its ability to live fully is inextricably bound to time-space, to body surroundings enfolded in all of living time. As your experience of harmony with space deepens, you'll cease reacting to spatial environments as "objects" which your rational mind must research, manipulate or control. You'll sense the "rightness" of places—or their lack of rightness—in much the same way that your holistic mind has that special "all-about" knowledge of a loved person described in Chapter Two. And that's what I hoped to suggest by the phrase "holistic ecology." Marcel Breuer, the great Hungarian-born architect, pointed in this direction,

> Colors which you can hear with ears;
> sounds to see with eyes;
> The void you touch with your elbows;
> The taste of space on your tongue;
> The fragrance of dimensions;
> The juice of stone.

Unstable Space is Illness

The concluding sections of Chapter Four explored "gravity" and the "knowing" that *is* gravity. There we imagined the need for *stable space* as a prerequisite for the evolutionary development of holistic mind, forever to be bound to the flow of space-time.

Perhaps the most dramatic illustration of the importance of creating a stable harmonious space in humans is to be found in studies of autistic children and schizophrenics. Genetically-at-risk infants have absent or decreased responses to gravity. Learning and speech disabilities of non-mentally-retarded children are related to dysfunction of sensing stable gravity. Gravity plays a specific role in tuning up the general motor and cognitive functions of the central nervous system. Children with average or better intelligence, who have reading or learning disabilities, lack a normal concept of their body image in space.

There is a lack of perceptual stability in the world of young schizophrenics. This lack of sensory integration is related to dysfunctions of stable inner spatial imaging. For example, some schizophrenics perceive the floor as unstable, wavy or soft; these typical phenomena become acute when the schizophrenics move. Their movement causes sensations of falling through space, floating, spinning, being upside down. Schizophrenic patients complain of losing control if they move, of everything becoming a jumbled mass, of things seeming to swing and move like a fast series of pictures. They have similar experiences if there is a sudden noise or too much noise. This suggests that schizophrenics have difficulty creating stable images of space, or trouble communicating that space to the conscious mind. Remember, the first requirement for the life of a cell was that bound mental knowing of up-down.

Whirling, head and body rocking, and head swaying and rolling are all typical behaviors of autistic children; these children do not get dizzy. This may mean that what is called "dizzy" is the normal experience of the autistic child and the chronic schizophrenic. They have learned by various types of feedback strategies to deal with a dizzy, unstable space much as a ballet dancer learns to control dizziness when doing turns by fixating. Autistic children have learned not to fall down by constantly living in an unstable space similar to dizziness.

Living Space

Let's return to the story of George, the hunter in our research investigations. He was a graduate student, with all of his life ahead of him. He was magnificent in perceptual relations with his spatial surroundings. However, these surroundings included people as well as space. Now George came up against the limits of the world of bound super-animal mind he had discovered. It didn't include the next step of living in a world with people. He couldn't feel a stable relationship with other people although he had a stable perceptual relationship with space. He was brilliant and a loner. A member of the Sierra Club, he would escape through backpack trips by himself to wilderness areas. He was comfortable in the wilderness as he never could be in society. He felt a deep intimate relationship with wilderness surroundings: rocks, trees, plants, animals. He would find himself enfolded in all the time of the evolution of that place. His bound mind could take over in wilderness space but not in social space. However, from his participation in the research investigation, George had learned that this bound mind's evolutionary development of stable space was the foundation upon which social relations had evolved. Human society is also time-bound in the hunter's world.

This is how the experience changed George's life: When he was in the wilderness feeling comfortable with his nurturing mind and intimate with his surroundings, he would substitute in his mind a person he knew who was like a particular tree, then another person who reminded him of a nearby rock. Soon he reached the point where he could surround himself with people while in the wilderness. He began to understand that other people also have holistic conscious-bound minds like his and that these minds are similar to the minds of the animals and trees of the wilderness.

George's rational mind is still isolated socially. However, his bound mind can now encompass and keep stable the social space of the other conscious-bound minds around him. He can feel intimate and immediate with others even though he doesn't know how to deal with their rational conscious identities. George lets identities clash around him. That doesn't disturb his harmonious social space. He's become quite popular. Others feel comfortable with him even though he doesn't conform to their social standards.

I also had to face at this time the incomplete nature of my experiments. This bound, holistic world enfolding time and space still represented only a small reduced potential of all that humans could be. In attempting to validate this experiment, I came to realize my rational mind was slipping in, abstracting and simplifying. The holistic mind does much more than perceive a world of space and time to which it is bound and immediate. It is spatial but also imagistic and stimulus-bound in contrast to the unbound, rational mind which has evolved differentiated, linguistic, linear, and sequential functions. In the next chapter we will go into ways in which this unbound rational mind can open the gates to a body-bound world of immediacy and passion through the conscious use of images. We will build upon George's experiences.

I know from my own experience that a man's life work is nothing but a long journey to find again by all the detours of art, the two or three powerful images on which his whole being opened for the first time.

Albert Camus

VI

IMAGE

Alice's Spiritual World

Alice is an old-fashioned name, and she was an old-fashioned lady. Alice was ninety years old. A broken hip had brought her into the hospital, a very common malady with women her age and easily fixed. At ninety, Alice's hair was still black with just a touch of graying. Her skin was still smooth. How was this possible? I began with her serene eyes. They encompassed me rather than saw me.

She didn't have any particular desire to talk to me. I got most of this story from a neighbor who was visiting her in the hospital and from her surviving daughter.

Alice had had as hard and stressful a life as one could have. The frontier of West Texas had been her childhood home. She had hidden under the cut bank of a creek when the Comanches had attacked. She had been hungry and cold. Her father died young, and she had helped raise the other children. Her own children, eight of them, had been born close together. Keeping the ranch going was hard. She once suckled a tiny baby lamb who had lost its mother. Two of her children died violently; two died of childhood illness. Her own husband had died early as had her father. Her last surviving child, the daughter, had brought her to the big city when she was eighty. She was supposed to live with the daughter and her family. Without their knowing exactly why, Alice's family found themselves going along with her wish to live in her own little cottage in a poor neighborhood.

Alice was incredibly healthy when I saw her. Her veins were on the outside of her muscles, just under the skin, like an athlete's. Yet, she had never jogged or swum or bicycled or done anything to keep her body in shape.

She had never taken vitamins or eaten health foods. She had never tried to control her health. Yet she healed rapidly. The nurses said she was the perfect hospital patient, quiet and contented. Around her was an atmosphere of being in harmony with her surroundings. She was quite clear and precise about her feelings but never seemed to have ideas about what she would get from the hospital. She would tell the nurses short little stories, but no one ever felt she was taking up their time.

Think back for a few moments about Ralph and Ruth, whose story appeared in Chapter Three. Through the power of his rational mind, Ralph tried to control his body and his environment. Alice, on the other hand, was in harmony with her body, and she intuitively and irresistibly gravitated to an environment with which she could be in harmony. Her rational mind moved only within this overwhelming pattern of harmony.

I drove out to see Alice shortly after she left the hospital. Pulling up in front of her cottage, I noticed it had an old-fashioned wide front porch. The walk in front and the yard were littered with tricycles, balls and other childhood playthings. She was sitting on the front porch in a rocker. A group of young children were sitting around her on the porch and on the steps, their faces turned up to her. She was looking off into the distance, not paying particular attention to the children. Then I noticed she was talking and singing a little. Some of the time she would just sit quietly. I couldn't interrupt and break the spell.

I went to see her neighbor. She told me that this was a

daily occurrence. "She's never invited them over as far as I know," she said; "She doesn't give them cookies or anything like that."

The neighbor told me that when the children reached six or so, they were no longer interested in her afternoon sessions. But up until six she was the pied piper and baby sitter of the neighborhood. "They're little animals before six," the neighbor said, "there's no keeping them still usually, but they're still when they're with her. They can't stay away from her."

"There you have the answer," I thought, "her bound, super-animal mind is communicating with their little animal minds. When their rational minds begin to take over at about six, they drift away." Alice is not important in the way Ralph was; but there she sits to this day, rocking on her porch and, merely by her presence, helping young minds develop their potential for living in complete harmony with their surroundings.

Ralph's superb rational mind had made him important to his society and his race, but he had irrevocably blocked his nurturing bound mind. If he had started in time, Ralph might have had the long healthy life Alice has without compromising the power of his great intellect. The balance is a delicate one; but perhaps we can learn to keep that balance in our lives.

We can live long and fully with both our rational minds

and our holistic minds. The holistic mind, time-bound and body-bound, wants to lead us into a world of images. But in order to do this, our bound imaginal minds must be allowed to express themselves fully. Alice lived with the nurturing images of sight, sound, smell and touch. Following is an experiment which will allow you to check your experience of these images to see whether I am misleading you.

Imaginal Experiments

At this point in the book we have experimented with how the holistic mind is embodied and is also embedded in surrounding body space-time. We have experimented with how to walk or jog in harmony with that living space which is the biosphere of the earth. With this preparation we can experiment with bonding body to image in what I call "imaginal space." Following are the research directions one subject in my experiments followed:

> Lie down with a pillow under your knees and get as comfortable as you can. If you can't lie down, sit down comfortably. Let your awareness drift over some of the dreams you have been recording. If other images appear, pay attention to them too. When your mind settles on a particular

dream, let the dreamscape become more
vivid and spatial. Wait; be passive as at a
concert. Let the feeling tone of your body
image in the dreamscape grow. Now
SHIFT and let your rational mind check
out your physical body: neck muscles tense,
eyes, mouth, shallow breathing, con-
stricted throat, tingling in arms or legs,
vague funny gut feeling, heart or blood
pounding, perspiration. . . . ?

If there are no noticeable physical body changes, go on
drifting with changing body images.

Imagine you arrive at a body-image change that is associated with a physical change. Suppose your right leg
feels tense.

SHIFT your focus of attention wholly to your leg. Let
the physical tension increase until it stops.

Then **SHIFT** back and let your body-image in space
happen. That image is now bonded to your body.

It may surprise you; you may no longer be in the same
dreamscape; your body-image in space may not make sense
to your rational mind; it may be a fleeting impression; or
it may be just where you were. You may hit it in the first
shift or the fifth. Don't spend more than fifteen or twenty
minutes on the process. If you haven't found a bonding
experience in that time, let it go until another day.

Usually a bonding between body, time and image happens this way: Your holistic mind has reached some resolution of itself. You can tell because there is an all-about, whole feeling similar to the feeling of a loved one you experienced in the second chapter. Sometimes you reach this bonding directly. You "just know" when you encounter an image that is bonded to brain, body, and time-enfolded surroundings.

If the bonding doesn't happen, here is a short three-step routine which will help: (1) drift through images, (2) check physical body with rational mind, (3) back to imaging—and you may be able to detect a difference between what I am calling a bonded image and the images which had previously been running through your mind. But remember, you are the experimenter. Do not be misled by me, or by the experiences of others described in this book. The image and physical feeling may be transitory, hardly noticeable, but go with what you have. As the experiment occurs more often, your sense of whether or not there is a difference will become stronger.

The body-image in space may make no sense to the active rational you at all. It isn't supposed to, just as a dream isn't supposed to. All you want to do at this point is to be vividly aware of the bonding of body-image in space and the physical feelings that go with it. Make a note or sketch of it on your record. This record will still record dreams and the waking, spontaneous experiences of your bound mind, but now it will record a more important level of living, your waking disciplined focus on the bound mind.

Examples

As an example of this process, here are excerpts from research transcriptions by Tom, the burly businessman whom we first met in the chapter on dreams.

> I'm flying . . . trying to fly . . . struggling; it's night . . . moonlight. I seem to be sinking . . .
> **SHIFTING** to body. My arms are tired, my shoulders . . . I'm letting that tired feeling build up until I just can't go on.
> **SHIFTING** back to dream image. I see the moonlight glinting off a roof below . . . a house . . . yellow light from a window.
> I want to let myself sink down and look in the window. In the yard . . . parents' yard . . . house . . . parents' house . . . frosted window . . . yellow light from the window falling on me.
> I'm standing . . . funny sensation around my waist . . . some kind of centering . . . centering of me . . . Oh! I'm flying. No effort . . . I'm all together . . . my center

. . . just floating, no effort . . . I'm just
drifting over the land. I can see valleys and
rivers . . .

It doesn't seem to me that my body image in space is changing anymore. I think
I've reached a limit, a bonding.

Yes. That feeling around my waist . . .

In this experience Tom achieved a bonding on the second shift of images. Notice that after the waist-centering-
floating-body image in space, there was no further whole
kind of change. Space was changing: rivers, valleys; but
the whole body-image in that space wasn't changing. Now
listen to Tom on another occasion when dreams weren't
used.

I'm just letting random images drift
through my mind. Nothing comes . . .
White tiles . . . floor. I'm about two feet
off the floor. Can't see my shoes. Looking
around . . . Pews. That's all. Black and
white tiles.

SHIFTING to body. Tension in my
neck and shoulders . . . pressing on my
shoulders and back . . . down. Tension in
my knees. Tensions building up; no force;

everything else relaxed; being with those muscles.

SHIFTING back to space. I'm pushing with my legs against that pressure. Black and white tiles. Oh! I'm floating, not standing . . . I'm floating up . . . in the middle of a cathedral. It's dim . . . an open door down below . . . light coming in . . . voices outside.

Nothing feels different. I'm just floating where I was. Oh, I can see my legs; they're kind of hanging down. This is my body position in my flying dreams and this was my body image in space the last time.

On both these occasions Tom arrived at a similar bonding limit. His two whole body-images in space were similar even though the spatial surroundings were different. Tom is finding what he is looking for, body images which have coalesced into a body-image in space key.

This was also my goal as I originally devised these experiments. I learned to be passive and wait. It took many times before my bondings of body-image in space began to coalesce into a coherent imaginal symbol which I could use as a key to the imaginal world.

What happens in a large research project like Tom's does not necessarily hold true for the rest of us. Much must be speculation. But if we come to true bonding limits of imaginal changes, and these images coalesce into an imaginal symbol, then you will have pushed your experience of your time-and-space-bound mind to an imagistic limit. Now you can differentiate between this bound experience and the limit of the most ordinary rational experiences of your self-conscious living. As you do this experiment over and over and record the results in your research record, you will be able to tell if the difference becomes more pronounced and vivid or gradually fades away. If the difference becomes more pronounced, then you may have arrived at a scientific truth about yourself.

You may now be realizing the same thing I did at about this point. At the beginning I was not able to judge whether or not I was being misled by my experiences because those experiences were such a small, rationally circumscribed part of all that I was. It is only to the extent that I become more fully alive, that I live more fully in my time-bound, space-bound and image-bound world, that I am able to become more purely myself. The truth of my scientific experiments depends on a fundamental change in my way of living. Knowing human truth as a scientist depends upon the extent to which I am fully alive to the potentials of being human. That is my research goal as a scientist and my life's goal as a human being. Come along on this quest with me.

As your life changes, your imaginal symbolic keys will need to change. You will need to keep checking on your feeling tones, but do not let these experiments turn into rules or procedures.

These experiments became part of my record and my daily life. I learned to call on my imaginal mind by activating an image in specific surroundings. Then my life began to change. I didn't change my life. I didn't have to do anything with that. But I began to be more fully alive.

What is being more fully alive going to do for you? There is not only joy. There is much suffering in the world, and as you live more fully you will become more a part of that suffering. The stories that follow will show what I mean.

Results

There are specific kinds of experiences that go along with this changed kind of living. Here is an example from the research record of a man who acquired an image of himself. The image was of himself standing in an unused, dusty room. He knew this was the room in which he grew up. It had his childhood furniture in it. Don't attribute any rational psychological meaning to this dusty, unused room.

It is bound to body and body-space and to all of time. It will not fit into any rational sequence of thought or identity, conscious of itself. It is a whole image, complete in itself, autonomous. Let me be clear; this was not a memory of a dusty room. This was a move into Freda's time, a way of living in a room that was a real room. His bound mind was bound to the time of that room. It still existed in his bound mind as truly as any room in his life.

Here is how this man used his image; he found himself in a job full of noise, hurry and confused purposes. He tried to deal with it in his customary rational linguistic way, but became increasingly tense with noise and confusion. This was not good for his health, so he realized he had a choice. He activated his childhood room image and suddenly everything changed. As he reported, "I can't really put this into words. It's, well something like this. At first, when all was confusion, it was like being in a room in which I was a guest. Then when I experienced the image, it changed. It was like opening a door into a room in which I was a member of the family. Now I'm a part of the noise and hustle, riding it and letting it support me. It is no longer confusing."

Here is another example from research records. A woman and her husband were about to buy a new house. She liked the house; it was striking and designed for efficiency. But she decided to see what her bound imaginal

mind felt about these new surroundings. First, she activated a body-image symbol of a musty smell in a vacation
log cabin in the woods. This was an image with which she
was comfortable. However, that image absolutely refused
to remain with her in the surroundings of the new house.
She became aware of an uneasiness with the house she
hadn't known she had. This was the kinetic image of
heaving roller coaster tracks. This image stayed with her
and she became aware of an acute dislike for her new surroundings. Her bound healing mind was saying, "Get me
out of here." They didn't buy the house. Her husband
understood. They were looking for a healing environment in which to live. Eventually they found a house which
furnished both of them with healing surroundings.

Sometimes people have used imaginal keys to become
aware of an actual environmental threat to their health.
Recall the burglar-in-house dream example from Chapter
Four. Sometimes dreams are very practical, immediate
warnings about your environment. Sometimes the healing
images act that way too.

Here are two examples of different uses of body-image
in space as imaginal keys. A very capable woman had become a member of the board of a small corporation. She
suffered a good deal of anxiety about her new role. On
top of that, the board meetings were acrimonious, and she
found that she could not get a word in edgewise in spite

of her ability to contribute significantly to the decisions of the board. The next time she came to a board meeting, she sat down in her chair and activated a body-image key to her bound mind. (Remember, the bound mind knows itself wholly and absolutely as it is. It cannot step back and be anxious.) For several meetings she sat there, passively centered and at ease with her surroundings with the absolute knowledge of her autonomous self. She made no attempt to be heard. Her rational mind still suffered the anxiety of its new role, but a pool of serenity and absolute confidence of her healing, bound mind began to spread out from her. Soon arguments weren't so disruptive; she began to be asked for her opinion. Now she switched to her active rational mind and contributed her valuable expertise to the board and the corporation. She found herself living fully, using both her minds at the right times. She also found she was feeling good.

A man working for a bank found himself running a construction job his bank had had to take over. His three-piece suit and obvious lack of knowledge about construction did not endear him to the construction superintendent and sub-contractors. He found his fiscal and contractual suggestions being sabotaged. So he stopped making suggestions and stationed himself every day on the job where nothing could fall on him. He found his physical body's center of gravity; he could stand there easily and confidently. Then he activated a body-image and stayed with his bound mind. Soon he found himself becoming aware of his structural surroundings and saw how it was all going together in a whole pattern. Soon he found that when deliveries weren't getting to the site or when sub-contractors were squabbling, he was being called on to do something. His passive whole sense of the job enabled him to know when to get involved and when not to. When he did involve himself he activated his rational mind. He pulled his bank out of a bad hole and found he was more comfortable with himself in general. He began to be fully alive.

These people were learning the appropriate use of their two minds. When everyone around you is panicking, say in a fire, keep your active rational mind completely in control. Your bound imaginal mind would run blindly and disastrously to get out of that unhealthy place. If you're in a different kind of crisis that calls for all your emo-tional and physical strength totally together in one effort, then activate your bound imaginal mind completely and let it mobilize your forces. For instance, you may have read the apocryphal story of the ninety-pound woman who lifted a car off her child. You will be surprised at how effective you can be in such circumstances.

The people in these examples were setting in motion inner changes which lead to a long, full, healthy life.

However, there are occasions when a healing image is directly connected to an immediate physical change. Here is a clinical case. A dancer had lost the use of her left leg. She had been a promising young prodigy before the condition gradually developed. There was no evidence of neurological pathology. The first step was for her to give up the idea of "curing" her leg; curing is a rational concept. She agreed to be content to get in touch with her leg. Her rational mind was not likely to be useful since it was not in touch with her body. Perhaps she could use a body-bonded image.

In a reverie, eyes closed, she reported images. I was using my brain wave equipment. Its computer showed a limit of the increase of brain waves in the right hemisphere, when she described a cliff, then a tunnel. She was asked to check her body. "My left leg is tingling," she said. In the next three sessions she explored these images, letting them build up to a limit of change. As she felt the limit approach, she would switch her attention and would become aware of her leg; then she would let that physical sensation build up to a limit of change. This switching would continue back and forth from body image to body sensation. Sometimes her leg would feel hot, sometimes cold. When she succumbed to temptation and speculated on possible "psychological" reasons for these images, she lost touch with her leg. Her bound imaginal mind had its own "reasons," which were not involved in her rational living.

She did regain use of her leg, but that was incidental to her learning to use her bound mind just to be in touch with her body. Another thing happened which was incidental to getting in touch with that mind. Her dancing improved. She began to realize how competitive she had been about dancing and how much anxiety and lack of confidence she had hidden from herself. Her rational identity remained competitive and anxious; that didn't hurt her as long as her healing mind was activated. Just the experience of opening herself up to her holistic, imaginal mind also opened her up to an enhanced sense of harmony of her body with space. Part of her knew her whole true self with absolute self-confidence. She had an imaginal key to that mind, which is conscious-bound to her body and her body's surrounding space-time.

Sports

This self-confident harmony with surrounding space can be experienced in any sport; just use an imaginal key. But remember, if you use that key to rationally control your performance, your rational mind will mimic your harmony with space. Then you will lose the confidence and grace that come from being bound to your body image and embedded in its surroundings. Use your rational mind for strategy and your imaginal mind for harmony.

One thing to recall: if you try some of these experiments with image keys, you must have some dreamscape experiences available to you. You may not have recorded any dreams at all; or if you did, you may not have become sufficiently immersed in your dream life to distinguish the surroundings of your dreams from the stories which your rational mind invents about them.

If this was the case with you, don't worry about it. Go through the experiment even if it doesn't noticeably work for you. Something may have begun to happen deep inside you. Each new experiment depends on your having fully enfolded the experience of your previous one, and it's very likely you won't be prepared for each new experiment. But that's alright. Go back to the old experiments when you feel ready for them. The process of expanding your personal experiments is circular. The result is the integration of your whole life; it must come slowly and passively.

Two suggestions: Before anyone tries this kind of personal research he should be sure that his feelings are flowing in that direction. Perhaps you say to yourself, "I should go through all of this because I want to live fully for a long time and be healthy." "Shoulds" cut your living off. Follow the experiments if you spontaneously, truly want to. Otherwise you are wasting your time.

Secondly, think about keeping your research record going. Especially record results. All these experiences grow together. You may find your research record of dreams changing to become the record of the whole life of your bound mind. In the next chapter that mind will be enriched by a lexicon of conscious-bound words.

The next chapter contains some experiments with bound words which enfolded (in Freda's kind of time) all the previous personal experiments in this book. The bound, imaginal mind uses words. In fact it has quite a lexicon of words. But it does not use these words as language. It is bound to its words. They are immediate.

Tom's Record
October 4

Peter complaining about my "smoking like a chimney"—"polluting" the meeting. Sense of being blocked—trapped—tried key image—didn't work—busted loose and let him have it—he right back at me. Messed up meeting.

Lunch—stomach ache—stopped eating—excused self and went out into park. Tried activating key image again—worked—I was exploding ball of light spreading out through park and city and atmosphere—went back to office feeling in harmony with everything like as they say, biosphere. Wonderful b.m., free easy—all of me—really let go. Wonderful. Rest of day good.

Dream—Railroad waiting room—brown, dirty—looking through dusty window in brown wall—lot of old ladies sitting inside. Slot in space and by being edgewise, could go through into room—Mother there in wheel chair—feeling of being edgewise in space.

We know with the head now, by the facts, by the abstractions. Why we are thus impotent, I do not know. I know only that this impotence exists and that it is dangerous, increasingly dangerous. I know that, whatever the underlying cause of the divorce of feeling from knowing, men cannot live and know and master their experience of this darkling Earth by accumulating information and no more.

Archibald MacLeish Sr.

VII

WORD

Unbound Language Versus Bound Word

"Do you take this woman here present to be your lawfully wedded wife, to have and to hold from this day forward?"

"I do."

This familiar language is immediately recognizable as the traditional formula for the exchange of marriage vows. It has been used for centuries, with slight variations here and there, not to "describe" the nuptial transaction between a man and a woman, but to effect and legally accomplish that transaction. The marriage vows are actually brought into being by this exchange: they are really bound to this formula, even though everyone recognizes there is much more to a marriage than that which takes place at the public ceremony, whether it be civil or religious.

Now consider this vignette, taken from the biblical book of Genesis:

> When (blind) Isaac caught the smell of Jacob's clothes, he blessed him and said,
>
> "Ah, the smell of my son is like the smell of a field that the LORD has blessed. May nations serve you and people bow down to you. . . . May those who curse you be cursed and those who bless you be blessed."
>
> After Isaac finished blessing him and Jacob had scarcely left his father's presence, his brother Esau came in from hunting. . . .
>
> His father Isaac asked him, "Who are you?" "I am your son," he answered, "your firstborn, Esau." Isaac trembled violently and said, "Who was it, then, that hunted game and brought it to me? I ate it just

before you came and I blessed him—and indeed he will be blessed!"

When Esau heard his father's words, he burst out with a loud and bitter cry and said to his father, "Bless me—me too, my father!"

But Isaac said, "Your brother came deceitfully and took your blessing." (Genesis 27. 27-35, NIV)

This familiar story about Isaac and his twin sons Esau and Jacob is also a stunning example of words that actually and immediately "do" what they "say." Jacob's blessing by Isaac was an absolutely bound word: its power and effectiveness, once uttered, could not be withdrawn, even though Jacob had shamelessly tricked his father and Esau's complaint was justified, since he was the firstborn twin and thus deserved to inherit Isaac's fortune.

Both these examples illustrate the power of bound words, words that are immediate, effective, reinforced by experience. They represent an absolute bonding of word with experience. This is opposed to the innate language mechanisms of the rational mind which are relative and grammatical. These rational language mechanisms depend on relative position in a linear sequence of words. This is the difference between whole pattern (or "Gestalt") and associative mental processes. Linear sequential language is based on a process of creating relations, a process of relative arrangement of words.

The holistic mind can understand many words, but it understands them as whole images bound to body and surroundings. It cannot understand them as sentences, as linear grammatical arrangements of words. The rational mind can only understand a word as a definition in a sentence. The understanding is of the linear sequential arrangement of the words, not the direct bound understanding of the holistic mind.

A grammatical rational word is unbound from direct body and body surroundings. Its conscious-of-itself meaning comes from its place in a linear sequential arrangement of other words. The meaning is changed when the linear sequence is changed. For example, "Mohammed came to the mountain" and "The mountain came to Mohammed" have profoundly different meanings, though both sentences use exactly the same words.

This chapter will focus attention on bound words, ones that speak immediately to the holistic mind, the words of exchanging vows, bonding, blessing and cursing. Bound words may take some getting used to. What you're reading just now are unbound, linear and sequential sentences that appeal to the rational self-conscious mind. Be gently aware as you read what follows that this rational mind will, as usual, want to analyze and intrude. It will try to search for meanings and hidden messages. Don't be dismayed; the experiments outlined here will gradually help you decide if you can verify these manifestations of your bound mind through your own experience and without being misled by that experience.

Breaking the Language Barrier

Bound words, like imaginal space, can be keys to being fully alive. Such words are bound to the whole pattern of body image in surroundings. For example, consider the sentence, "I feel depressed." This seems to be logical, linear language. But what about the words themselves? "I" is clearly rational; it refers to your self-conscious identity; "feel" implies a body sensing not readily available to your rational mind. "Depressed" is also a word not easily accessible by rational definition. Think of a time when you were feeling depressed. Now try to express this feeling to yourself in descriptive language.

          ❧   ❦

Don't you find it very difficult? You say, "There is this feeling in the pit of my stomach," or "My throat feels swollen." But you know these language descriptions aren't getting at the authentic feeling of depression. So you give up and say "depressed." Many books have been written about depression without doing any better. "Depression" is a way of being which can be clinically defined but is very difficult to describe in language.

Now try this; substitute "blue" for depressed.

Are you more comfortable with "I feel blue?" Does it seem more direct or immediate to your imagined feeling of depression? Try "down;" "I feel down."

Both of these words are spatial time-bound words. (Blue describes the spatio-temporal vibration of light.) Sometimes they become stripped of rational linguistic meaning and regress directly to the holistic mind of the body embedded in space. See if you can think back to a time when these or similar words became immediate, when they communicated an absolute revelation of your body sense in its surroundings.

If you can think of such a time, you are remembering when you broke the language barrier and, through a word, entered an absolute world.

You may say, "What you've been describing is just the use of metaphor in language." If you think what has just been described is metaphor, that may be why you haven't had the experience. For one thing, metaphor is a complex linguistic stategy which begins with an invitation to the rational mind and ends with an invitation to break the language barrier and enter the absolute world of the symbolizing bound mind.

Strictly on the surface, metaphor looks like a "mistake" in language, a conflict. If I say "the sea is dark wine," or "Juliet is the sun," I seem to be guilty of either a mistaken perception or just plain nonsense. Factually, the sea isn't wine, nor is Juliet a swirling hydrogen fireball. Whatever similarities may exist between sea/wine and Juliet/sun, the differences are greater. Metaphor's "mistakes" thus create conflict for the rational mind at the level of "literal meaning." In its effort to resolve the conflict, rational mind discovers it must surrender control over fixed and exact meanings, because metaphor's meanings are too multiple and too slippery. In short, metaphor confronts the rational linguistic mind with a barrage of meanings that are already wobbling out of control.

If the rational mind surrenders to metaphor's strategy, it will be swept out beyond the world of linear, sequential sentences and toward the world of symbols. And when that world is reached, one has entered the silent precincts of bound mind. Metaphor begins as "mistake," continues as conflict, forces rational mind to surrender control, and steers us toward symbol. "Juliet/sun" thus fails as rational expression, but gains the condensed, immediate and precise power of symbolic image.

This is, of course, what happens regularly in effective poetry. The art of poetry invites your rational linguistic mind to identify one thing with another. For example, "The color of the sea is like dark wine" is a sentence which rationally describes the color of the sea. But on the other hand, Homer found immediacy in "the wine dark sea." The "wine dark sea" breaks a linear sequential meaning to allow your bound mind to participate in the experience. The art of poetry might be thought of as the attempt of the poet to so arrange words that their linear rationality is broken through and a word comes to have that sudden immediacy, the revelatory bound quality of the time- and space-bound mind. Robert Frost said,

> The right reader of a good poem can tell the moment it strikes him that he has taken an immortal wound—that he will never get over it. That is to say, permanence in poetry, as in love, is perceived instantly. It hasn't to await the test of time. The proof of a poem is not that we have never forgotten it, but that we know at sight we could never forget it.

While the rational mind reads the poem, it is the holistic imaginal mind which takes the immortal wound. Words are relative to the rational mind; to the healing mind they are immediate, absolute and undying.

You have experimented in earlier chapters with distinguishing mental imagery from the imagery of reason. Now let's begin to distinguish bound words from words used sequentially by the rational mind. You will experience embodied words that are revelatory, that occur in song, poetry and prayer. And you will be able to experiment with intentionally revealing the experience of the healing word to yourself.

Word Experiments

There is a basic difference between using images and using words as keys to a full life. Bound images (Chapter Six) were experienced randomly while you were in a passive state. Your passive mind had no intention. You "just knew" the random emergence of images that led to a key image able to open the gate to the passive bound mind. Bound word experiments will occur through passive intentions of the bound mind itself; they are not random experiences.

Here is how it goes: Get comfortable. Close your eyes. Choose a deep, passionate intention, such as cutting down on your eating in order to be healthy. First, remove obvious, rational controls such as "cutting down." You're left with "healthy eating." Let the intention be while it becomes stronger and more passive at the same time. This seems contradictory, but you may be surprised at how strong an intention can grow if you hold it passively.

Holding the derationalized image passive, let single words drift through your mind until one seems to complete the whole passive intention pattern. Let us take the example "healthy eating." The completing word may not have any rational connection with an intention of "healthy eating." That's to be expected. Say the word is "yellow." This is a word which you "just know," is bound to your healthy eating intention. Your "just knowing" will depend on the passion of your intention.

The bound word is now embodied, conscious-bound to your body and your body space. In this case "yellow" is bound. Wait until the feeling tone of "yellow" becomes vivid and precise. Now switch to your rational mind and rationally use the word yellow in a sentence. Can you feel the difference?

❧   ☙

If you can feel the difference, you have a key experimental word ready to open you up to a healthy eating body in a healthy eating environment. Eating is a whole pattern of mind, body and surroundings. The word is directly bound to your body and eating surroundings. But remember, it will take many of these experiments to begin to determine whether or not you are being misled. You are in charge.

Say you use the word "yellow" which you have already embodied. When you sit down to eat, before you do anything else, activate this bound word key. It will be like saying grace. If you do say grace the key can go along with grace. You will experience a fleeting moment of spontaneous awareness of what is good for you. Let your spontaneity overwhelm your obsessions and conventions. Eat what you "just know" you want.

୶ଌ   ஜ৯

This is difficult. You may become panic-stricken at the prospect of letting go of control just when you are most committed to controlling your eating habits.

There is the real danger that your self-conscious mind will counterfeit your awareness of the bound mind. You may be saying to yourself, "Oh, I'm spontaneously hungry; I spontaneously love the taste of food; I spontaneously want to eat and eat; therefore it's good for me." That, on the face of it, is a counterfeit of your bound mind. You are not being spontaneously and fully alive but only aware of your identity-centered food obsession. You are

spontaneous after getting in touch with a bound, immediate word, not before.

Becoming aware of your embodied mind embedded in
its surroundings thus involves both discipline and the self-
emergent ordering of that mind. The "word experiments"
proposed here can help you discover those word keys that
open your holistic mind and make you spontaneously aware
of what you want and what you need. Since we've already
used examples related to eating habits and nutrition, let's
stick with those for the next few pages. Food is, after all,
an item of interest to everyone, especially in a world like
ours where well over half its people are hungry, while
others (Americans, especially) are obsessed with fears of
obesity. And since exercise is so closely linked to nutrition, we'll look into it as well.

Self-Regulation of Eating

You may find you do not want any of the things in your
food surroundings. At the same time you may be aware
of the rhythmic metabolic functioning of your organs and
"just know" you want something to eat here and now even
if it's not in front of you. This is like the experience of
the incomplete pattern of "houseness" in the third chapter when you left the tap running in the bathroom. Use
your rational mind to make a list of possible foods. Suppose

"apple" seems to fulfill the healing pattern. Eat an apple.

If it is what your body needs, you will be satisfied. You may still be bothered by compulsions to eat involved with your rational identity roles, but your bound mind will be satisfied. You will feel whole and healthy. You will no longer be obsessive about your weight. It is the very obsession with losing weight which makes losing it difficult.

Your Right Weight

What does it mean, being overweight: Over what weight? We all know that overweight is supposed to mean being over the weight of a statistically average person. But the statistically average person changes with fashions. What we are really expressing these days is a desire to be fashionably slim. Not all that long ago it was fashionable to be plump. Next time you visit the Metropolitan Museum in New York, take a look at Peter Paul Rubens's painting "Venus and Adonis." You'll notice immediately that Rubens painted in an era when a generous plumpness was perceived as voluptuous, beautiful. "Ideal" weights are just that: ideals of beauty or health that change substantially from one historical epoch to another and from one culture to another. Caution and even a healthy skepticism about such ideals is in order. What is considered a healthy weight for one person is quite possibly unhealthy for another. And any good physician will probably tell you the same thing.

A major life insurance company is publishing a revision of its tables of desirable weights. The new weights are from five to fifteen percent higher than in its last tables. Either the new tables are right or the old tables are. They can't both be right. In fact neither may be right for you.

You can discover the right weight for yourself by activating a bound word key. There is a fleeting moment in the presence of food when you "just know" what your body needs. This moment is often overwhelmed by compulsive habits and conventions before you become fully aware of it. By using a word key to your bound mind, you become fully aware of what you need.

But this key will not "cause" you to eat less or "control" your weight; those are concepts of the rational mind. These keys allow you to be more fully alive to what your body really needs to eat. To the extent your living changes, your weight will change to be right for you. One doesn't have an eating problem. One has a living problem.

If you go all the way with your bound mind, your body weight will eventually become what is most healthy for you at a particular time and in specific surroundings. It may not be the weight your rational identity demands; you may not fulfill the current fashion; you will weigh what is healthy for you. If you become obese or too thin, your autonomous body functioning has broken down; use your rational mind to tell you to see a medical doctor.

A word of warning—remember the fairy story where a magic word would get you what you wanted. In those stories of magic, getting what you wanted was sometimes disastrous. Recall once more the story of Jacob and Esau. Isaac's word of blessing was so laden with power that it could not be withdrawn, not even by the utterer. This is always the way with potent, bound words. You may get what you ask for; so be sure your original intention is pure. If you can't feel that way about your intentions, stop. Try again later.

Healthy Exercise

Everything you have experienced about full, vital living in this book has helped you to judge how and if your unique bound mind can do its own thing. Every effort by the self-conscious mind to control the body's health and healing crowds out the very mind which is doing the healing. For example, one reads that exercise is good for the heart—not necessarily. It may be bad for your health to take your heart out jogging just because you should, because your rational mind, conscious of itself, thinks it is responsible for and in control of your heart. Some people, even those in ostensibly excellent physical shape, die of heart attacks while jogging. The great James Fixx is a recent and tragic example. Other people exercise only enough to get from their chair to the table, and they never have heart trouble. Exercise is neither good nor bad. It is how, why, when and where you exercise that is good or bad for your health.

The walking or jogging we have been doing in harmony with the living space of your biosphere has been a key to living all the way. It is also healthy exercise. Perhaps by this time you have acquired the precise emotional feeling tone of this harmony. Give that feeling tone a word key. Whatever the exercise may be, it will then be harmonious, enjoyable and healing.

Health Rules May Harm

You are unique. You have learned how to let the embodied bound mind lead your own body into a whole pattern of health. But to do this runs contrary to the world of rules and statistics that flood the nutrition and health-care industries today. While such statistics are sometimes useful tools for interpreting large-scale trends or patterns in public health, they are usually too general for application to specific individuals. Statistics can't give you specific rules for your own well-being, nor can health regulations alone make you healthy.

Some healthy people, for example, eat health foods and

shop religiously for vitamins and supplements at nutrition centers. They might be perfectly healthy without health food, but if such persons are attuned to their environment, they may feel a spontaneous desire for health food. However, of themselves health foods don't impel those who eat them to be healthy. In fact if these foods are eaten primarily because they constitute an "ideal" or "rule" for good nutrition, they may actually crowd out the holistic, bound mind which ultimately regulates body functions. Health rules can crowd out vital living. Your holistic mind is specifically bound to your body embedded in its surroundings here and now. When it is functioning harmoniously in whole patterns, it knows what is best for your own health in each specific time and place. There's no need to try controlling your body with reason or to try "fixing" it with logic; simply be in harmony with the living space of your biosphere. Only you can know what is healthy for you. No one can write general health or exercise rules that apply specifically to you. Be aware of your bound, nurturing mind; spontaneously participate in its harmony, wholeness and healing; but always check it out with your rational mind. There may be something wrong with your body which needs professional medical attention. If so, don't hesitate to call a doctor.

Self-Regulation of Smoking

Stopping smoking is currently fashionable. Stopping or cutting down on smoking is not a bad idea, even though some people lead long satisfying lives while smoking. You can try to control smoking with your rational mind, conscious of itself. But have you noticed how tense and irritable you get? Try turning smoking over to your bound mind. Take the time to embody a key word bound to your smoking body in your smoking environment. Like all aspects of a full life, smoking is involved in the entire self-emergent pattern of your living. If you smoke and want to stop, bond a word to your intention to stop smoking, following the procedures you used to discover the right eating habits and the right weight for yourself. Be sure your intention is pure before you proceed.

Say the bound word is "nicotine." When you reach for a cigarette, activate the word and open the door to your bound mind. Smell your fingers, imagine the tasting, smelling, lung and blood feeling of inhaling a cigarette. Does this fit in with the total pattern of your holistic mind?

❧   ☙

If it does, take out the cigarette and smoke it. It's conceivable that smoking here and now is doing something for you. But if you don't feel the positive tingling completion of a healing pattern with the imaginary cigarette, then don't smoke it. You may have a self-conscious identity dominated by the compulsive urge to smoke the cigarette anyway, but don't you still feel good and fully alive not smoking it?

Remember what the Surgeon General says, "Cigarette smoking is dangerous to your health." I say the same thing. Be suspicious of any feeling tone that tells you a particular cigarette at a particular time is healing. Your rational mind may be counterfeiting the feeling tone.

Some people say, "Taking all that time and disciplined ordering of just one desire to smoke a cigarette is not possible within my lifestyle." Anyone determined to preserve and control a comforting lifestyle should avoid this book. Living all-the-way is a total discipline, full and harmonious. Keep it up and your lifestyle will surely change.

If one has a smoking problem, the problem isn't smoking. The problem is living. You don't have to change any one thing, just your whole life. Let me put this into three steps: (1) Give up. Surrender the control strategies of the rational, self-conscious identity; (2) Get in touch with the bound mind; and (3) Once in touch with the bound mind, your lifestyle will inevitably change, and other changes in diet, exercise and smoking will self-emerge from the more fundamental change.

This self-emergent quality of changes from living with the bound mind as well as the rational mind point up again what this book is about. Experimental results with human beings must self-emerge from our experiences. If we attempt to control conditions for results, we know less about human beings because we are less fully alive. Are rational boxes of quantified measures about controlable parts of human beings more precise knowledge of humans? Can one cram human beings into preconceived rational boxes? I think not. Are you beginning to feel that images and bound words give you a precise self-emerging knowledge about your whole self which your fellow human beings can also know and share with you?

Words/Wounds

Bound words, potent and inexorably effective, are, more often than not, challenges to change. In the early pages of this chapter Robert Frost spoke of poetry as a wounding experience. Poetry wounds, as does all genuinely revelatory speech, because it breaks down the defenses which our rational minds, so preoccupied about preserving self-identity and control, strive to build. Ironically, those defenses prevent the very thing they appear to promise: a fuller life, happiness, spontaneity, harmony and wholeness. There are lines near the end of Rilke's famous sonnet, "Archaic Torso of Apollo," which express this point exactly.

> . . . .there is no place at all
> that isn't looking at you. You must change your
> life.

As the sculpture of Apollo wounds the viewer—demands change—so Rilke's poem wounds the reader. Be sure that you check your intentions before seeking those key words that give you access to your bound mind. For that mind, despite all its potential for healing both human body and human spirit, is not a simple garden of earthly delights where one stops to smell the roses. Quite often the bound mind will confront our rational, self-conscious identities with a forthright ultimatum for change. What we can be sure of is that if such a demand is made—and if we have become genuinely aware of the feeling tones and images from that "other" mind—we will not be misled and the change, however painful, will not do us harm.

That is why the deepest human words, characteristically expressed in prayer, poetry and prophecy, are very often wounding words. But those wounding words heal. A famous passage about Israel's "suffering servant" from the biblical prophet Isaiah is an illustration.

> He was despised and rejected by men,
> a man of sorrows, and familiar with suffering . . .

> But he was pierced for our transgressions,
> he was crushed for our iniquities. . . .
> and by his wounds we are healed.
>
> (Isaiah 53.3-5, NIV)

This example is especially interesting because in a single text all three expressions common to the bound mind are present. Isaiah's words are poetry, a piece of his larger message of prophecy which, in turn, is set in a context of worship and prayer. The prophet's point is a wounded/wounding one, much like Rilke's in the Apollo sonnet. Seeing the disfigured yet God-favored and mysterious servant (a holistic image, not one aimed at rational analysis), Israel is beckoned to change, to abandon the illusory pursuit of power over its own destiny and future.

The way to living fully with all we are and can be requires enormous courage because it demands a vast openness to change. Key image-words, bound to body and environment, are thus keys to change— not only to changes in health-and-nutrition habits, diet, exercise, smoking and a host of other popular "causes," but to far-reaching changes of heart and spirit. Religous persons have ordinarily labelled such changes a "conversion," a revolution in attitude, behavior and life so complete that a new mode of being results. While this book is not religious, it does propose disciplines and routines which, if followed, will affect every aspect of your living. Archibald MacLeish's words, which introduced this chapter, may also serve to conclude it: "Men cannot live and know and master their experience of this darkling Earth by accumulating information and no more."

Tom's Record
September 26

Notice sleeping less and feeling more alive. When get tired, I'm really tired, all of me—and I conk out completely. Harder to fool with dreams.

Family freaked out over saying grace at table—only way I can use key word. Beginning to get a sharp solid feeling. Letting it do its own thing.

Dream—bed—huge—sick at stomach—hot—clammy—sick all over—corner of room—window on each side.

Writing this down, I know this is Mother's bed. I remember—she is saying to Doctor—"You see what happens when this child overdoes." Hear the sound of her voice. Vivid.

. . . . A man: who, knowing his whole true self,
cannot be used or possessed by any power other
than himself, and whose life therefore is lived for
life's sake and never in the service of ruin, or
pain, or hatred, or the dark.

Ursula K. LeGuin

VIII

EMOTION

Sailing to Byzantium

Byzantium, Constantinople, Istanbul: three names for the same city, names that shimmer and swirl with smoky minarets, exotic food, bazaar-jammed streets, roasting coffee, daggers and intrigue. Built, like ancient Rome, on seven hills rising from both sides of the Golden Horn, an inlet of the Strait of Bosphorus, old Byzantium was possibly a stop on Jason's journey to fetch the golden fleece.

Modern poets have been able to sift through the enfolded layers of dust and light to catch for a glancing moment the symbolic center that is Byzantium. William Butler Yeats, for instance, in "Sailing to Byzantium,"

> Once out of nature I shall never take
> My bodily form from any natural thing,
> But such a form as Grecian goldsmiths make
> Of hammered gold and gold enamelling
> To keep a drowsy Emperor awake;
> Or set upon a golden bough to sing
> To lords and ladies of Byzantium
> Of what is past, or passing, or to come.

Yeats's images are themselves redolent, aromatic, stimulating. They appeal less to the rational analytic mind than to the bound, imaginal one. Feeling tones predominate over intellectual ones; we sense immediately the silken decadence of a bored imperial court that cannot hear itself crumbling to destruction.

Yeats uses body-imagery and time-bound body-space to wound and challenge readers. The physical surroundings of the poem become charged with emotion. And we can respond because our holistic minds recognize space itself as a quality of emotion rather than a physical "thing" to be emptied or filled.

A visit to modern Istanbul is an illustration. The great domed church of Hagia Sophia is less a space or an object of dramatic architecture, than a charged emotional event. Like the archaic Apollo of Rilke's poem it wounds us with the demand "You must change your life."

Space is Emotion

I find that my personal sense of space is one of the strongest stimuli to my emotions. When I say to someone, "You're on my turf," I can also feel a surge of emotion come through me.

But I find it difficult to put those feelings into words. I feel emotionally aroused, but I can best express that feeling in words bound to space. When we say "turf" we probably mean our social turf, but the social turf was derived from our territorial instinct. All animals defend their territory. We do too. Territoriality is one of the most basic motivators of our being, and it is expressed emotionally. All our relations with space are expressed in precise emotional feeling tones.

This precision comes from our spatial surroundings. Remember the feeling tone that told you precisely "all about" a loved one in the experiment which opened Chapter Two. No computerized meter can do as well. This feeling tone is absolute, and it is emotional.

Absolute Emotional Feeling Tone Versus Relative Knowing

That knowing all-about a loved one which you experienced was an emotional feeling tone. It was precise. You could feel the whole pattern go click. An artist or a poet has an emotional feeling tone that goes click when the right color or the right word falls into place. The composer, too, "just knows" when the tone-color, rhythm and voice-leading are "right" because the whole pattern of the composition has clicked into place.

Conscious linguistic knowledge is relative; one is conscious of its linear sequential coming into being. One can step back from it and examine the logical premises, test it for consistency. Inherent in this knowledge is the possibility that a different sequence could make a different meaning and thus yield a different knowledge. There are few scientific laws of natural order which have not changed since they became knowledge.

Absolute Knowing

There is little absolute knowledge today, no absolute right or wrong, no values that are absolute in rational systems of thinking and talking. There is no way of knowing absolutely who one is. Identity has become a personal crisis managed by any one of a vast and growing number of psychological systems attempting to make identity rationally and consciously consistent and under control.

Not so very long ago there seemed to be much absolute knowledge in the world. One did not possess it through a logical process; one "just knew it." It was revealed. At a deep level, one knew precisely who one was; and in living, this conscious-bound self was constantly revealed and enriched. This self was never discovered, never depended on rational identity for existence, and so never suffered any crisis or depletion.

Emotional Evolution

George the hunter's rational discovery of his identity as the great hunter was relative. But George, when allowing his bound-to-environment mind to occupy all his attention, had precise absolute knowledge of who he was, what he was doing, and where he was. He was bound to his body and to the life of the forest where he hunted. His volition and his conscious-bound self were revealed to him in the whole pattern of what he was doing. He was the time-bound space around him and the event of his kill within that ground of space.

As Blaise Pascal remarked in his *Pensées,* "La coeur a sa raisons que le mens ne connait pas," "The heart has its reasons that the mind does not know." We have measured the holistic bound mind in the electric potentials of the right hemisphere and the whole body; it has become clear that this mind is bound to the heart, the muscles and the rest of the body. It is also bound to the emotions.

Emotion seems to be related to the limbic areas of the brain at the bottom of the skull. The evolutionary remains of these animal brains in human beings express emotions, species personality, and bound words. This is the communication characteristic of bound mind. These primitive areas of our brains cannot control the fine motor requirements of the tongue for human language; their impulses must be mediated by right brain functions. The left cortex seems to be unable to accept the existence of functions associated with the lower part of the brain. Only the bound mind can mediate emotion-formation impulses.

Emotional Communication

Emotional communication is thus separate from verbal communication. For example, the left side of my face (which is connected to the holistic, bound mind) is dominant for communication of my emotions. It expresses emotion more intensely than the right or rational side of my face.

I find there are two distinct and separate ways I respond to facial cues: a delayed choice (rational sequential analysis) and the instant unitary choice of bound, holistic mind. Facial expressions, you may have noticed, are the prime communicators of emotion. Emotion is very difficult to describe verbally and cannot be remembered well in language, as you've perhaps noticed from your experiments in dreams. Emotional states are non-dominant, not part of a sequential, verbal stream of experience.

Emotional communication is structurally distinct and separate from sequential language. A sergeant in the army had a stroke which destroyed a portion of his right hemisphere. He can no longer communicate the feeling tone of anger. When he tells his troops, "I'm mad as hell," they don't believe him. He can say he's mad in language, but his right hemisphere is no longer able to open the gates to his body expression of anger. That's a bad situation for a sergeant to be in.

And it's a situation quite different from that of Patricia Neal (Chapter Three), whose stroke had damaged her left brain hemisphere. Pat had an experience opposite from the sergeant: she felt and knew emotional tones absolutely, precisely, but could not, prior to her recovery, express them in verbal language.

Fear and Anger

Emotions are foreign to the rational conscious mind. This mind fears emotion. The body-bound mind is where emotions exist. We use words such as anger, fear, love and hate to express emotions. But our emotions themselves, even though precise, never quite fit those words. I notice that my rational mind, conscious of itself, often doesn't know whether to laugh or cry; that a relationship may be love or hate, and my rational mind isn't sure which it is.

Rational culture has taught us that emotions are sloppy and ambiguous. But you may have experienced emotional feeling tones through this book as the most precise experiences you can have. Emotions are not ambiguous; it is the labels which the rational mind tries to put on emotions which are ambiguous. The labels don't fit. The rational mind talks around and around emotions without ever being able to simply describe them. An emotion cannot be stuffed in a rational box.

Have you ever tried to analyze (rather than feel) an emotion such as fear or anxiety? You say to yourself (or to your therapist), "What caused this? Where did it come from? What is the sequence of events which preceded it?" The more you analyze, the more vague the emotion becomes. Like a dream, it slips through your fingers in the talking. What you have left is a rational narrative, isolated from the actual emotion. Soon the rational mind has closed those gates on your world of full living which it fears and which it cannot express in its own terms.

We can repress and even direct our behavioral expression of emotions with our rational conscious identities, but we cannot control the existence of these emotions. Think of someone with whom you are angry. Try to bring that hot emotional feeling tone back. Is your heart beating faster, your breathing faster?

৵৽   ৶৶

Now try to release this anger by explaining to yourself consciously and rationally why you are angry. Does this calm you down?

৵৽   ৶৶

Check your heart and breathing. I expect it has made you more angry. Imagine you are trying to release the anger by rationally explaining it to the person with whom you are angry. It might go something like this:

(A) "I've been very angry with you. I want to explain to you what it was you did that made me so angry."

(Suppose B also believes in a therapeutic system of releasing anger.)

(B) "Don't dump that garbage on me. That really makes me angry. Let me tell you what it is about you. . . ."

Or A might try expressing A's anger to B violently. Then A may get a mouthful of B's knuckles. Aren't you even more angry?

In spite of psychological beliefs to the contrary, releasing anger consciously through a therapeutic system often feeds anger, makes it destructive. A humorous example of this occurred in the film "The Four Seasons." In a memorable scene, Alan Alda and Carol Burnett have travelled to their daughter's college in New England for a "Parent's Weekend." The autumn foliage is breathtaking, searing scarlets and rich yellows, the sky is that royal October blue, the air is crisp and fit for football. Everything about the weekend promises to be superb. But Alan and Carol, though hardly aware of it, have embarked on some profound discoveries about themselves and about their marriage. Alone in their guest room at the college, they begin a perfectly rational discussion along the lines of "You tell me what about me makes you angry, and I'll tell you. . . ." Reason gradually gives way to rage, agreeability to anger, shouting and abuse. What began as a calm reasonable discussion of anger feeds the emotion to the point where it flares utterly out of control.

Later in the same film a similar episode occurs in a vacation cabin where Alan and Carol and two other couples have gone for a winter weekend. They decide to be "totally honest" with each other about their emotions, with disastrous, if comic, results.

The Critical Distinction between Emotion and Behavior

Emotions have come to fall within the province of mental health and psychotherapy. In therapy the repression of emotions is often thought of as harmful. Yet you have just experienced how the expression of anger can actually intensify anger and make it even more harmful.

Many troubled people are helped by psychotherapists. Psychotherapists are, after all, human beings devoted to caring and helping in every way they can. But psychotherapeutic theory of emotion in itself has not been as successful. Traditional psychotherapy has said, "It's O.K. to let go of your emotional behavior. Nothing bad will happen." But bad things do happen. This psychotherapy has failed to make the critical distinction between emotion and behavior. Emotion exists in the world of the bound-to-the-body mind. Control of behavior exists in the rational mind. Emotion, of course, impinges on the rational mind, but the rational mind has no way of processing it. It puts names to emotions, but the names become ambiguous and unsatisfactory.

Healing Emotion

Here is the situation. Repressing your emotions is bad for your health. Expressing them without control feeds back upon itself. It is just as bad for your health. It sounds like a catch-22, but there is a way out. You can control your emotional behavior with your rational mind so it won't feed on itself, and at the same time you can turn the emotion itself over to the holistic mind where it lives. Either of these ways by itself can be disastrous. Only if you do them together will this solution work. But you still have to experiment with this solution yourself.

You have been experimenting with how you might live with all you can be, all the way, in passion and power. In the next section you can try this by using both your minds in the highest and best way that each can function.

We have been preparing for this experiment with experiences of body-bound images and body-bound words. We have experimented with image-keys and word-keys to open the gates to our bound mind.

Image can be seen; word can be said. Rational consciousness can hold on to them while learning to trust the absolute and precise nature of emotional feeling tones. Perhaps through your experimentation you have come to rely on a precise emotional feeling tone to tell you when an image has become bound or a word has become bound. But emotional feeling tones in themselves are inaccessible to rational consciousness. To experiment with your emotions you must acquire the courage to consciously be with your conscious-bound mind without your rational, self-conscious mind suffering a nervous breakdown from having lost control. With the experience of image and word, we are ready to move to what we can neither see, hear nor say—the emotional feeling tone itself. Indeed, to do this takes courage, but it is not more than we can do. As we have "just known," we can also "just feel" our emotions.

Have you ever seen a strong emotion, such as love, fill someone up until they glowed? What were they doing? Nothing. They were passively allowing the emotion to be. If they had actively expressed in behavior what their rational mind understood, they would have lost the full, free experience of that emotion within the whole pattern of their living.

Emotion Experiment

At this point we should be ready to experiment with passively allowing emotions to be, without trying to repress their existence.

Try anger. It is an easy kind of emotion to practice with. Let the original hot feeling of anger come back. Accept that feeling tone as it is, without words or images. Next, let it expand through your entire body, toes, finger tips, scalp, gut. Use your rational mind to control behavior; this frees your holistic healing mind. Let the emotion freely expand through you until you can feel yourself glowing. Your body's radiance has increased. Let yourself glow. You no longer need to use the abstraction "anger."

◦⟳⟲◦

Have you experienced your emotion in all its uniqueness as a precise feeling tone immediate to your mind and bound to your body? Can you tell the difference between this experience of anger and either acting-out anger or repression of anger?

Have you reached a point where your two minds can express a whole pattern of themselves? Use bound words and images. Break the language barrier. This is akin to what goes on in poetry and art.

I find that my emotional feeling tone of anger changes when I can turn it over to my conscious-bound mind. It becomes a part of the whole pattern of my living. Why would I want to get rid of this feeling or express it in behavior? It has power; it's comfortable to live with. Perhaps it will eventually merge into the stream of my life and disappear, but I don't have to worry about that. I have used my rational mind to do what it does best, control. And I have turned the emotional feeling tone over to my fully living mind to be absorbed for what it is, as it is. I've neither denied the emotion's existence nor intensified its destructive potential by "acting-out" behavior. I find this to be an important step toward integrating emotions freely and fully into the whole pattern of my life.

Spontaneous Emotion Experiments

Now that you have experimented with having a complete emotion that is neither repressed nor "acted out," see if the same thing happens spontaneously in your living.

One can't control when or how an emotion will happen, but one can prepare for it. Take the time now to walk or jog around the block in harmony with the living time and space of your biosphere.

                          ≈

Was the feeling tone of the experience emotional? Did you know precisely when it was there? I find this kind of walking or jogging will tune up my emotions. Overwhelming emotions become comfortable. On the other hand, when I am unable to feel passion, the walking or jogging releases it. I can feel tuned up emotionally at precisely the right balance. Then I am ready to experience a spontaneous emotion.

First, here's something to do with your knees. They also have a special relationship with space and healing emotion. Have you had the experience of getting up to speak and finding your knees are trembling with emotion? Or have you had someone tell you how their knees buckled with emotional fear? The muscles on top of your legs just above your kneecaps resist gravity and hold your knees from buckling. I think of them as my emotional muscles, bound to space. Find a place to be comfortable and relaxed. If you can lie down, put a pillow under your knees. Now pay attention to those muscles on top of your legs just above your kneecaps. Be passive. Don't let them tense up; keep them relaxed, but pay attention to them. You may feel a slight tingling. Don't try to do or accomplish anything; just be with those muscles for 15 or 20 minutes. You may find your breathing has altered slightly, that it's happening lower down and with less effort.

Sometime during the next few hours, or perhaps even the next day, I find that I will experience a spontaneous strong emotion. If this happens to you, have the courage to transform it to a healing emotion as you have just done with anger. Enter the experience in your experimental record. Emotions repressed by rational mind without being transformed to their precise, absolute expression in our holistic, fully alive mind are bad for our health. We all have these emotions which we haven't transformed to healing emotions. Keep yourself open to these buried emotions and, when you can, transform them to their healing expression. This will not hurt you or anyone else. Keep up the walking or jogging and the knees routine. It will help make your repressed emotions available to your healing mind until you reach the bottom of your emotional barrel. It may take a long time.

You can be free to live with passion, with excitement, to keep your emotional feeling tones bright and clean. Emotions are inner experiences. Leave them to be freely and fully experienced. Discipline your rational mind to inhibit their rational expression when such expression is ineffective.

Laughter Experiment

When you have the hang of this kind of experience of emotion, once you know the emotional feeling tone, you can go directly to a full body experience of all your emotions. It works even better with joy and love than with anger or fear. You will be surprised how effective this passive expression of emotion can be. If you keep experimenting with images and immediate words as keys to your emotions, you will find your emotional feeling tones becoming precise rather than ambiguous and vague. You will know them fully.

Be on the alert for any feeling of emotion however fleeting. You may be surprised at how rich an emotional life is being lost to you every day. If the rational mind can't linguistically identify a transient emotion it will ignore that emotion.

Here is my suggestion for a research design. Try setting up some image or word keys to alert you to emotional feeling tones. Colors seem to work best for me. At the same time build a rational discipline for your rational mind. It doesn't have to be able to deal with each emotional feeling tone. Your rational mind can leave it up to your body-bound mind to passively feel the emotion. As an example, we sometimes feel filled with the joy of living. Sometimes a laugh will just bubble up from deep down in our diaphram—a belly laugh. One's whole body comes into tune. At this point the body-bound mind is passively expressing itself.

Then, when the feeling tone of this laughter is fully felt, let your rational mind, conscious of itself, take over as it did when you described a loved one. Express the laughter consciously directed to the "reason" for this laughter. Explain the laughter in words and rational action. Does this remind you of waking up from a dream and telling the dream? See if you can tell the difference. As an example, I find I can always tell the difference when my laughter is directed at someone. Then it has a reason attached to it. The mind conscious of itself is now in control.

The word "discipline" has cropped up several times in this section and in the preceding ones on "Healing Emotion" and "Emotion Experiment." It's important to understand that the process of discovering emotional feeling tones demands attention, work and the disciplining of the rational mind so that it doesn't inhibit genuine contact with emotions. This is especially difficult today, when the image of a "liberated" man or woman is one that promotes "letting it all hang out," consciously abandoning all rational inhibitions so that "true self-expression" can occur.

As we've seen, this approach can be an invitation to disaster. The way to full, free emotional living balances both a passive allowing of emotions to be *and* an active control, by rational mind, over how, when or if these emotions are expressed. That's why the distinction between emotion and behavior is so critical. Emotion exists in the world of the bound-to-the-body mind; control of behavior exists in the rational mind.

Self-Regulation of Stress

Stress and stress-management are the subjects of many sets of rules in today's "mental health market." Hans Selye did the definitive research on stress. He identified the General Adaptation Syndrome as an overloading of normally self-regulating hormone functions. Some people have had their health damaged by stress, while others have survived places as horrible as Auschwitz. Stress is not harmful in itself. Don't be afraid of it. Live all the way with what you've got. It's "how" rather than "how much" that determines if healthy stress turns into an unhealthy General Adaptation Syndrome. When you are in a stressful situation, you can appropriately activate a word or image and give yourself a little zing. Then you will find the stress healing and exciting. Stress can actually increase your resistance to illness. Being relaxed in the midst of a full life is fine. Being relaxed to tranquilize stress is a rational identity syndrome. It's not living fully, and it's not good for you. Your holistic bound mind is your friend and wants the best for you. The rational mind must learn to be friends with this whole, healing you. It must learn the joy of living all the way and must use the tools for bonding limits of change. Life will become simpler. Wholeness and healing will extend all through you.

Going All the Way

Family therapists and marriage counselors have been seeing the increasingly disastrous condition of couples who seek to solve their problems by rational arrangements and contracts which exclude the holistic bound mind. However, those whose rational minds can allow their bound minds to go all the way, to be immediate to one another spiritually, are healed and free to love with joy. They are no longer responsible for making love work, for controlling love.

Parents, too, these days feel responsible for "Parenting." Rules for "Parenting" crowd out the expression of the encompassing love emerging from living with all you've got with both minds. Whether with a lover or child, your rational mind clutches in panic at the prospect of "going all the way" with another person. That means risking your controlled, self-conscious identity. Indeed it often happens that a person will become so dependent on another that they will subordinate their rational identity to them. Sometimes they don't get it back. Don't do that. Use your rational mind to control your identity; after all, identity is the creation of the rational mind. It is a constant and terrible responsibility. But that responsibility belongs to your rational mind. Leave it there.

Then use a binding key to your bound mind and go all the way with another in wholeness and joy, full of faith and love. You can't lose your true self, for it is bound to body and surroundings, to all life and all time. It is absolute; you can't lose it. You can't lose.

The Destructive Responsibility for Illness

Alice, whom we met in Chapter Six, is the only person I have known who did not have either a rationally repressed or distorted emotional component to her illness. Both illness and emotion are ways of being in the world. They are inextricable one from the other. But, as Alice did, it is possible to turn the emotions of illness over to our bound super-animal mind to be experienced fully as they are. When that is done, healing results that are often startling will follow.

It is so easy to feel rationally responsible and guilty for our illnesses. Do you sometimes feel that if you had controlled your body more completely according to some system of mental health, diet or exercise, that you would not have become ill? That is your rational identity speaking. Your healing bound mind knows better.

Illness is not a dragon waiting by the side of the road to devour us. Different illnesses are different ways of being in the world. Some of these ways are less comfortable for us than others, some are less conducive to long life than others.

Leaving out being broken or crushed or burned, illness is not a simple effect of some cause which is exterior to us. Medical doctors follow linear sequences of steps by which they discover symptoms of illness. A symptom is simply a reduction of a patient's specific experience to an abstract category, to a rational box. A certain linear combination of these rational boxes is the diagnosis of a specific illness or disease. This kind of medical diagnosis is one of the most productive results of human art and science. We must all thank God every day that this kind of system is available to us. It works. It saves our lives and makes us more comfortable.

But no thoughtful medical doctor confuses the symptoms of an illness with the illness itself. The illness is a total pattern of the body, mind and environment. For example, many patients with illnesses such as tuberculosis, pneumonia, meningitis can change these ill ways of being in the world to a more comfortable and productive way by killing bacteria in their bodies with antibiotics. But the various bacteria associated with these illnesses have not "caused" the illness. Some of these bacteria are to be found in our bodies most of the time. Illness is a total way of being in the world. When you are ill, be with your healing bound mind. And see a medical doctor.

Freedom and Illness

Say you become ill with something simple like a sore throat. You've seen that medical doctor, and you've also turned your sore throat over to your healing mind. In a few hours you may notice the warm pulsing feeling of blood flowing through the sore area of your throat. You begin to feel better. Your rational mind says, "Oh, I've learned to control my blood flow." And your rational mind will concentrate on keeping the healing blood flowing.

In a short while the warm pulsing will go away. Your rational mind will say, "Oh, I did something wrong," and it will scurry around looking for a new theory. By that time your body-bound mind is completely shut out.

Notice that the healing was already going on when your rational mind began trying to seize control. Don't let this happen. Have faith in your bound healing mind. Let your illness be in harmony with your body and body surroundings and the whole living space of your biosphere. You are no longer responsible. Revel in your freedom and harmony. Your illness will, in its own time, be absorbed into the wholeness of all life.

However, sometimes your illness is so overwhelming that it can only reach a harmony with life through your death or disability. When you are ill, it is time for your rational mind to take over and direct you to a medical doctor.

Humankind has always known its potential for healing, for living all the way; it is ancient human wisdom and scientific consensus. It is so basic we fail to realize the distinctions involved. The problem has been how to disentangle the bound healing mind of emotions from the active, rational mind so that precise measurements could be made and a scientific dialogue begun.

My personal experiments seem to have come to a dead end with my emotions. I am a long way from reaching the bottom of the barrel of my unassimilated emotions. Until I do reach that bottom, I'm not sure how to go on. It seems I've been following a research direction rather than a research design. The experiments of dream, space, image, word, emotion have flowed continuously from each other, have found their own direction and meaning out of their need to be validated and enfolded in ever more whole experiences. I had thought that this direction toward wholeness would end in a final validation which would enfold all the reduced partial experiments along the way. That was to be the next and last chapter.

But I see now that such a validation can never be. Living fully can never have an end when we can say, "Now I'm fully alive." There is, after all, an arrow of time through which we are forever becoming, changing, and enfolding all that has ever been and still is. The most and the least we can do is try to keep up with this becoming.

There will never be a point at which I can stop and enfold with a final experiment all the experiments which have gone on before, thus validating them all. This is so because time is always moving into the future. There *never* will be a point at which I can stop time. If I commit myself to experiments which continuously enfold other experiments I can never stop. Validation can only be achieved when time is constrained within rational boxes. When evolving life is made static, it becomes an illusion of our rational minds.

I do not have an experimental design for the next chapter, but we must go on. I propose to exhort you with a random collection of tales and ideas. Perhaps some one of you, my readers, will find, self-emerging, the new research direction we all need.

Tom's Record
October 9th

Peter did it again to me this morning—I got so mad I was about to bust—and it worked for the first time—activated key—could feel that anger seeping into every part of me, arms, fingers, hair—think my hair must have lifted a little—just looking at Peter with all of me mad—I was riding something—I didn't have to do anything—I could see Peter trying to get mad like he always does. Then he tried to laugh—then he looked uncertain. Stayed focused on him the rest of the meeting—not a peep out of him—Ha—Did he leave in a hurry after meeting.

While driving home, word key popped into mind— "blue"—sense of stillness—image of clouds—no wind.

Mary trying to protect John from me again at dinner. Makes me so mad. After kids in bed started to have it out with her—but from her expression, headed for a big fight.

Shut mouth—Let it happen again like Peter—Worked—Tingling all over—Tingling turned into sex—Mary too—Wow, sex into love—slept in love.

Dream—Desert—sun—rocks—thirsty—tired—desperate. Big bird wheeling overhead. Closer—I'm trying to keep going—staying with it—Bird right over me—Sudden switch—soft, warm, huge mound. Blots out everything—I'm sucking on a nipple—safe, warm. Instantly gone, but I was at my mother's breast.

Don't tell me this dream hasn't any rational meaning. Oh—rational, but more than rational. Feel it more now—but no words for it. Tired of words.

Then will the eyes of the blind be opened and the ears of the deaf unstopped; then will the lame leap like a deer, and the tongue of the dumb shout for joy. Waters will gush forth in the wilderness, and streams in the desert; the burning sand will become a pool, the thirsty ground bubbling springs.

Isaiah 35.5-6, NIV

IX

SPIRIT

A Problem with Mind

We have all grown up breathing a cultural atmosphere which insists "mind doesn't really exist; it is just a word for brain functioning." After all, we think, where is mind when brain is destroyed or dysfunctional, while the body still exists? The tragic example of Karen Ann Quinlan comes to mind. Years have gone by since she lapsed into a coma after an overdose of drugs and alcohol; yet she is still considered "alive" even though life support systems have been removed. The operations of her left and right hemispheres—which we can observe and measure—have ceased. Her rational mind, conscious of its own functioning, has ceased. What is left? Only that part of her body-bound mind exclusive of her right hemisphere seems to remain, because her vital functions, breathing and heartbeat, continue to be regulated naturally.

In Karen Ann Quinlan's case, consciousness, both bound and unbound, has ceased to exist. Does that mean that this young girl no longer has any mind at all? The question is more complex than it may at first seem. As we have discovered by experiments throughout this book, the bound mind—quite distinct from the rational, linguistic one—is bound to *all* the cells of the body except for those of the brain's left hemisphere. As long as those "cellular body minds" exist, then bound mind still exists and its binding to body, space, time and environment must still exist. Karen Ann Quinlan lacks a rational mind, but a part of her body-bound mind is still living.

The troubling case of Miss Quinlan raises questions for which neither science nor philosophy has fully satisfactory answers—as witness the controversies which surrounded her parents' decision to remove their daughter from life-support systems. Can the discoveries we have

made in the experiments suggested by this book provide
any help? Can we achieve greater clarity about the relationship between our two minds and about what of us
survives the events we ordinarily link with death?

The Mental Life of Cells

Follow life back through evolution as brain becomes
smaller. What happens when brain disappears? Does bound
mental existence then disappear? Does this mean that an
organism with no brain has no bound mental existence?
What about those organisms with only a spinal chord?
Many actions such as jerking your hand from a hot stove
are expressed in the nerve cells from the hand to the spinal
column and back. Brain as such is not necessarily involved. But isn't this a function of bound mind, whose task
it is to organize body cellular functions? What of organisms with only rudimentary nerve fibers? Do they have
mental existence? What of cells with no nerve fibers?

Today we can answer these questions by performing a
rather simple experiment which requires only looking and
seeing. Imagine you are looking through a modern micro-
scope. You are watching a living human cell divide. The
actuality is very different from textbook descriptions. The
action of the chromosome fibers duplicating themselves,

the new pair moving to the opposite side of the cell, the cell pinching itself in two in the middle, and then jumping apart as two new round cells—all this takes the time to count one, two, three, jump. Feel the joy of that bouncy jump; feel the sexual nature of that release.

Shift gears, now, and watch a white blood cell at work. When white puss oozes out of an infected cut, that is millions of white blood cells coming to fight an infection. Watch one white cell moving along inspecting other cells to see if they are healthy. It does this by stretching out and moving itself over the other cell membranes. Notice first that the cell is moving, second that it is moving under its own power, third that it is using its own judgment about the direction in which it is moving, and fourth that it is using its own judgement about which cells to inspect and which to pass by. Suddenly it stops, moves all over another cell. This other cell is a cancerous one. The white blood cell backs off, hesitates, then throws itself at the cancerous cell and destroys it. If the white cell identifies more cancerous cells than it can handle, it will soon be joined by other white cells. Cooperatively they will try to destroy the cancerous cells.

In both these examples cells behave as if they had minds of their own. They seem to "think," react, feel and communicate. The cells exhibit a power of interaction that confounds explanation at the strictly chemical or molecular level. It is a power we can only describe as "mental" life, as non-material activity.

❧   ☙

Now that you have performed this experiment, check yourself. Isn't your rational mind trying to explain away the obvious mental life of these cells? Perhaps you are thinking, "That white blood cell was just chemically and electrically programmed to do that." It is true that the white cell is stimulus-bound to its surroundings. It is bound to respond wholly to body stimuli to try to identify and destroy diseased cells and foreign cells. But who "programmed" it? The white cell is not connected to the brain. It receives no instructions from the brain.

Or your rational mind may try to think of the white cell as being a different, separate organism which your body has. No, this cell results from the dividing of those two original cells which were you at your conception. This white blood cell has its own separate bound mental existence, as do all the cells in your body. It is not programmed; it is not a computer. It is bound to evolution and to space-time. It partakes of that bound mental existence, unattached to any brain, which is characteristic of *all* that is, from the squiggle of amino acids in the primal sea, to the proto-cell, to complex cellular organisms, to the bound mind of humans which *does* have a relation to the brain's right hemisphere.

Over billions of years a social colony of cells, each with its own independent mental existence, has evolved bound together spiritually to be that bound mind which organizes your functioning from the brain at the top of your head, through your organs and muscles, to the tips of your toes. Our bodies are millions of mental existences! Though she neither speaks nor reasons, Karen Ann Quinlan is a living being abounding in mental existences.

The Touch of Immortality

The cells of your body die but they can also be immortal. How can this be? Say a cell divides into an "A" and a "B" cell. Say "B" cell dies. Does this mean that the original cell has died?

⅓   ⅆ

The question just raised is like asking if you're still beating your wife. Or like the famous query posed by Zen masters to their novices: "What is the sound of one hand clapping?" In this case how does one tell whether "A" or "B" is the original cell? Either could be the original cell.

Suppose "A" divides into two other cells. As long as any one of the ensuing cells exists, the original cell exists.

Who can say the existing cell isn't the original "A" cell? As long as only one cell of the millions of cells of your body survives, then all of the cells of your body live. Which was the original cell? Does the question really matter? If even one cell of my body survives, do "I" survive, does my "self" survive?

The bound self never dies because cells never die. In contrast, rational mind needs the brain to survive. When the brain dies, so does the rational self as we ordinarily identify it. But the bound self never dies; it is a "holon-archy" of all the cells in the body, including the right hemisphere. Through evolution cells have changed as their function has changed, but the original cells continue living just as we still live even though we have changed. If all cells died, if ever there were a complete break in ter-restrial cellular life, there would be no more life and no more mind. There could be no renewal. When a person dies there is a cellular renewal. Our cells change as our living changes. That change remains.

This is not much comfort to your rational identity. It will die. Have you in your experiments, experienced identity as a construct of the rational mind, unbound from cellular bound mental existence? It is precisely because the rational mind is *not* bound to cells, body, space and all that has ever been in time that its identity constructions will not survive. But your cellular extension through time is the touch of immortality. And consider, your bound mind with its touch of immortality is at least as much a part of your everyday living as your rational identity is. If we do not blow all life up, your bound self may extend indefinitely into the future. Your bound mind has to do with your touch of immortality.

Immortality Experiment

Just as your cells are mentally bound cooperatively to your whole body and surroundings, so are all your organs such as your heart. Have you ever had an experience which was disastrously dangerous? Stop reading for a moment; go back and try to relive your body feelings.

_&_   _&_

Didn't your heart start pounding and your whole body move into alertness for action before your rational mind, conscious of itself, even knew there was a crisis?

Your rational mind might be saying, "Oh, I was conscious of that at the same time I moved. I couldn't detect a difference." That's because your rational mind won't admit the existence of your bound mind. Your rational mind exists because it has learned to step back and put bits and pieces of itself and its surroundings into a linear sequence. That is the only way it can be reflexive, conscious of its own functioning.

Take another pass through your dangerous experience. Your rational mind, conscious of itself, would have had to reduce that situation to parts, then put the parts together in a linear sequence before its special kind of consciousness could be aware of the crisis. Do you think your rational mind could have done this as fast as your holistic healing mind, which is bound to the whole pattern of the crisis? Your heart knows about your environment before your rational mind does.

Psychic Healing

Jesus Montoya is a friend of mine. I use the Spanish pronunciation, Hay-soose, because calling my friend "Jesus" in English makes me a little uncomfortable. Jesus is a carpenter and also a faith healer. His extra time and money go into faith healing. He owns a big revival-type tent and goes around to different towns healing people.

I want to tell you how he healed me, but first I'll have to tell you about another friend of mine, one of the very best bone doctors in the world. I came to him with my wrist broken once and he said, "You've made my day. I can put this in a cast and it will heal. Everyone else I've seen today is in agony and I don't know how to help them."

Later I came to him with a damaged foot, and he said, "OK, this time you've done it. You've lost the cartilage on the ends of those little metatarsal bones and I can't put it back. I can straighten it out and set the bones, but you will never walk normally again." A year later I was getting around very well with a cane and was resigned to the fact that I would always have to depend on it. It had been romantic at first, but now I was getting bored with the reality.

Then Jesus came by one day and said, "Come on. God is going to heal you." I went with him, although, of course, I didn't take it seriously. At his revival meeting Jesus took my foot in his hands and prayed. I was surrounded by people who believed. Jesus' hands began to get warm. His body glowed. I could feel the radiance. Jesus knew a miracle was going to happen. I was appalled. I, a scientist of mind and body, was here under false pretenses.

The miracle didn't happen. There I was, surrounded by expectant faces.

I was seized by a sudden irrational impulse and threw my cane away. I turned and walked out. It hurt like hell, but I made it to the door and after that to my car. I haven't used a cane since. I kept telling myself I was going to buy a new cane, but I never did.

I still don't have any miraculous cartilage on my foot bones, but I am now walking. I can even jog a little bit. I don't consciously or rationally know how I am doing this. My holistic healing mind, bound to body and space, does know. Apparently, there are ways I have aligned my body which don't put stress on those bone joints.

Heart Knowing

Let me go back now and put my experience in terms of my own speciality, using electric potentials of brain and body to study the mind-body link. I mentioned that Jesus' hands got hot and that he "glowed" much as you have experienced glowing in internally focused emotions. I can measure this "glowing" in your body's electric aura. However, I must tell you that Jesus' electric brain waves would not have shown any decisive correlation with "glowing." Research attempting to show correlations between brain waves and psychic phenomena, such as healing, have been inconclusive at best.

Here is where we have gotten off the track. We have failed to make the distinction between rational mind, unbound from body and surroundings, and the holistic healing mind, bound to body and surroundings. The electric aura of the rational mind is from brain waves, but the aura of the holistic mind must be measured in electric potentials of the whole body (including the right brain hemisphere).

For example, when Jesus was "glowing," his whole body aura was dramatically increasing even though his brain waves were not. His arteries and veins were increasing in size and the majestic electrical pulse of his heart was spreading through his entire body.

Nothing was happening to me, but Jesus was bound completely to his body and his right hemisphere. The psychic phenomenon which was occurring was inside Jesus, not between the two of us. What did happen was that Jesus' experience and the whole environment of the expectant crowd gave my holistic mind permission to take over the problem of my foot. Whatever else psychic phenomena may be, they are an interior experience linked to the whole binding of mind, body and environment.

You may have noticed I have been using the words "psychic phenomena." The "psyche" in psychology is a Greek word meaning soul, or the spirit of life—that immaterial breath which, through humankind's long history, has been thought of as the difference between clay and life. So why haven't I used the simple English word "spirit?" For the same reason I call Jesus, "Hay-soose," instead of the simple English pronunciation of Jesus. I find myself uncomfortable when I use "spirit." Perhaps you do too. Let me use the word spirit for the body-bound mind.

I have called this mind so many things throughout this book: conscious-bound (conscious but stimulus-bound to brain, body and surroundings), so that it is not conscious of itself; primal, super-animal, nurturing, holistic, healing, mute (not able to speak language), imagistic, dream-like. I have used all these words because I am confused and uncertain about how to express this mind in language. The development of language in humans has by its very nature denied the existence of this other mental world. However, since the mythic time of the sealing off of Eden, when words became unbound and available for language, there has existed this bound word, spirit. It has been a container for all the linguistically ambiguous qualities of the body-bound mind. This word (in whatever language) has been spirit. Perhaps this spirit is simply all that is not conscious of itself, not manipulable and linguistic in human beings. However, the healing passion and power which I am trying to experience in this chapter must be called what it is, spirit.

Spirit

There is a big problem here. I am using "spirit" as something to do with being bound to body and space and time, and all life that ever has been and ever will be. But our scientific and secular culture tells us that spirit is the *opposite* of body and time and the living ecology of our surrounding space. The only thing we will admit we know about spirit is that it is unbound from body, environment and time. But is that really true? I am discovering just the opposite.

The rational mind has talked and talked about spirit from the dawn of human history. Still there is no rational agreement as to what spirit is. Novels and poetry grope after it. You know when you have touched spirit, but can you put into rational words what it is? Language throws up imitations of spirit: duty, oughts and shoulds, systems of religion, morals and ethics, relationships which can be controlled. We know in our hearts that these are not spirit. Isn't spirit the same substance of which dreams are made? Doesn't it slip through your fingers when you try to capture it rationally? Holistic mind is bound to body, space and time. Is spirit the binding? Is spirit that which binds all body-bound minds together and, further, binds them to all times and spaces that have ever been in the evolutionary history of life's living cells?

When I first tried to think of a personal experiment to investigate this question I found I couldn't even consider it. I had blown my rational mind. It was like the Zen question, "What is the sound of one hand clapping?" It has been hard enough to experiment with the truth of the bound mind, but to consider the truth of the binding of all bound minds. . . .

I am still groping, however. Later in this chapter I recount an experiment which I finally tried. The results, while still ambiguous, seem to indicate that this binding is the opposite of everything I thought it ought to be.

The more that rational mind has taken over our lives, the less reality has been left to that linguistically ambiguous, silent, unattainable binding. Less and less is evoked in us by the word "spirit." Indeed, the more rational mind, conscious of itself, has taken over the world, the more embarrassed we have become by the word "spirit." It seems empty, forced, as when we halfheartedly lament the decline of "school spirit" or "patriotic spirit."

The exceptions are to be found in poetry, literature and art. The binding I have called "spirit" can express, through artistic breaking of the language barrier, the conscious bound world of the holistic mind. Such moments—which occur often in great poetry and painting—are acknowledged by humans everywhere as spirit, "spiritual." Still, the rational mind will want to dismiss artistic image and invention as unreal or as mere idle decoration. Wallace Stevens was keenly conscious of this conflict between the bound mind's expression of a *whole* world and linguistic mind's compulsion to dissect and analyze that world, to control it through the artifices of speech. In "Less and Less Human, O Savage Spirit," Stevens wrote:

> If there must be a god in the house, must be
> Saying things in the room and on the stair,

Let him move as the sunlight moves on the floor
Or moonlight, ...

It is the human that is alien,
The human that has no cousin in the moon.

It is the human that demands his speech
From beasts or from the incommunicable mass.

If there must be a god in the house; let him be one
That will not hear us when we speak: a coolness,

A vermillioned nothingness, any stick of the mass
Of which we are too distantly a part.

Forever restless and discontent, linguistic mind fears
letting spirit be spirit, wants to force this "god"—this in-
effable binding of all that is—to speak, to take on shape
and color which rational intelligence may then *name* and
control. Propelled by an instinct for dominion, an instinct
it senses cannot be fulfilled, rational mind insolently demands that beasts talk, that the incommunicable communicate. It cannot rest content with the bound words of
spirit, which we met in Chapter Seven, nor with the "vermillioned nothingness" of dreams which dry up like jellyfish on a beach when they are "translated" into a rational story.

Some very great human thinkers have shared this insight with poets like Stevens. I remember, many years ago, running across a thin little book by Josef Pieper entitled *The Silence of Saint Thomas Aquinas*. Both the size and the title of the work intrigued me: such a minuscule volume on such a voluble churchman! Thomas Aquinas's collected works, after all, fill a very large shelf in any library. And even today, more than seven hundred years after his death (in 1274), his voice and name are heard not only in churches and divinity schools, but on university campuses all over the world. Many a college freshman has to struggle with at least a tiny bit of his thought in a "Western Civ Survey" course.

How in the world could Josef Pieper write about Aquinas's "silence?" I read, and found out. I also continued my own experiments and discovered for myself how this prolific medieval philosopher and teacher could, at life's end, ask his young protege to destroy his greatest work, the *Summa Theologiae,* because, Thomas said, it was nothing but straw. Was this great man merely acting humble, masking the kind of pious, self-effacing gesture expected of saints on their deathbeds?

My own experience tells me that Aquinas's "last request" was a serious one made by a thinker who had profound insight into what it means to be fully human, fully alive. Historically, Thomas Aquinas lived at a watershed moment, shortly after Western Europe had made contact with the cultural richness and diversity of other peoples as a result of the Crusades and the opening up of trade routes and commerce with the Middle East in the twelfth century. One important consequence of Europe's "Twelfth Century Renaissance" was its rediscovery, largely through translations and commentaries by Arabic scholars, of ancient Greek philosophy. Works of Plato and Aristotle, long forgotten in the West, became available once more, and intellectual innovators like Aquinas began making use of them. From that moment forward, the unbound rational mind, whose evolution in the West had been partially slowed and stunted by the so-called "Dark Ages," began developing very rapidly once more. It was the threshold of that epoch in human evolution which we like to call "the Modern Age." The apparently limitless reaching-out of rational intelligence was on a roll, a roll that has continued 'til our own day of nuclear fission, quantum physics, space exploration, artificial hearts and DNA-splicing.

Like others of his era, Thomas Aquinas prized the wild restlessness of intellect, its appetite to know—and to *know* it knows. He pursued its ways vigorously, ascribed to rational mind and language a power of moving towards ultimate reality (which he called "God") that revolutionized traditional understandings of such things as "revelation" and "truth." The power to receive "God's revelation" was, Aquinas argued, a capacity built into the very structure of human life. Such realities as "truth" or the "ultimate" in value and meaning no longer needed to be construed as "objects" existing outside the arena of human possibility. A fundamental *unity* existed between human beings and Ultimate Being—and thus no dualist explanations were required in order to affirm the intimate link between humanity, world and "God."

But Aquinas's work did not stop with the celebration of human intelligence and its restless potential. He sensed, though he did not elaborate it fully, that intellect is inhibited and that language is limited. Quite significantly, his most mature work, the *Summa,* begins not with an arrogant display of how much we humans can rationally know and say (in this case, about God), but with a setting of limits, a subtle discussion of the "breaking point" in knowledge and discourse, that frontier beyond which thinking and speaking are useless and, indeed, insignificant. Had he been familiar with modern research into the brain's hemispheres and the mind/brain relationship, Aquinas might have spoken about the limits of unbound rational mind in relation to the limitless "knowing" of the mind bound to body, space and time through the whole course of evolution.

In any event, Aquinas seemed to sense the bound mind's silent wisdom. He recognized that rational mind's restlessness is not an end in itself, but a key to unlocking those

"Gates of Eden" that allow entry to the world I have described as "spirit." Built into the very structure of existence—built, I would say, into the very origins of evolving life from amino acid molecule to multi-cellular organism—is a kind of "undertow" that pulls us forward and binds us not only to one another, but to all times and to all life in our universe.

So my astonishment at the title of Pieper's book on Thomas's "silence" was resolved. The silence of Aquinas was the silence of the bound mind, living fully on the threshold of that world of spirit which is the binding of all life that was and is. It is that world—spirit's world—which Wallace Stevens hints at so strongly in bound images "incapable of speaking, closed:" light, color, shapes, coolness, a "vermillioned nothingness." Spirit is the binding that silently and speechlessly, unites the whole web of life from its beginnings until now.

The Web of Life

Darwin came to a remarkable understanding of life: that we were not created complete as we now exist, but that we evolved over billions of years from individual cells. Then his rational mind, conscious of its own functioning, had to scurry around to find a linear sequential explanation. He came up with natural selection which became known as "survival of the fittest."

I can feel comfortable with "survival of the fittest" as I can with "Hay-soose" instead of Jesus, or "psychic phenomenon" instead of spirit. My identity feels comfortable because it has imposed its own linear sequential order on life. But evolving life existed long before rational mind became unbound from its environment. Evolution is not linear sequential cause and effect. It is bound, and spirit is the binding.

Evolution is not merely the gradual self-emergence of biological organisms but also the self-emergence of the bound mental organization of those organisms, everything from squiggles of amino acids to human beings all mentally bound together in Freda's all-inclusive time. What we normally think of as brain had nothing to do with this evolution. Nevertheless, evolution has been a *purposeful* becoming. "Natural selection" and "survival of the fittest" can be seen only as constants of a rational mind forever alienated from this evolutionary Garden of Eden.

Watson and Crick have decoded the RNA and DNA structures of cells. We know a good deal now about cells, their genetic codes and how they reproduce. But "survival of the fittest" has shielded science from having to confront the understanding of how individual cells form organisms like us.

How *do* individual cells form organisms like us? Science has no understanding of this. The understanding must come, as the understanding of bound mind comes, from our accepting the existence of two separate mental worlds, the bound-to-environment world and the unbound rational world. Evolution exists in the bound world. Understanding the evolution of life can only come through experience of the cellular binding of spirit.

Here is a slime mold organism, for example. We can find it on a forest walk as a slimy amorphous mass shining among the scuffed-up humus of the forest floor. But where is the organism? It isn't there. All we can find is a bunch of individual cells eating up all the organic matter in their environment. When the food is gone, one cell or a number of cells secretes a chemical communication. Does it matter whether the communication is linguistic or chemical? It's still mental communication. The cells all locate each other in space, and separately and autonomously decide on a central location and congregate there. Then they cooperatively create a little tree with a bud on top which holds the cell chosen to produce the next generation of slime molds.

Can a rational argument like "survival of the fittest" help us understand how these cells cooperate? No. But the experience of love and compassion as being more than rational identity can lead us to know spirit as the binding force of the cells which have sacrificed themselves to make the slime mold tree. It is the same self-sacrificing binding of cells which made us. Are love and compassion qualities of the bound mind rather than the rational mind? Experience tells me they are.

Think of a herd of grazing animals, antelopes for instance. To protect against predators the most fit antelopes stay on the perimeter of the herd. When the herd is attacked they are the ones least likely to survive. Yet they give their lives for the survival of the herd. Human beings have gone to war throughout history. Who dies? The most fit. But their love and self-sacrifice survives in the spirit of humankind.

There is no controller. There is no rational law such as "the survival of the fittest" which controls our evolution. There is a bound world within which the evolution of life takes place. If you can experience this other mental world, you can be in touch with the original cells of the beginning of life and your cells of possible future life, with the alpha and omega of all you are.

Our rational minds understand the material composition of our cells very well and understand our bodies very well. But rational minds have no answer to the one crucial question of what life is all about:

> How and why do individual cells with bound mental existences of their own co-operate to form human beings?

Perhaps the answer is spirit. Let me repeat the quotation which introduced the third chapter of this book.

> That, while we are thus away, our own wronged
> flesh
> May work undisturbed, restoring
> The order that we try to destroy, the rhythm
> We spoil out of spite: valves close
> And open exactly, glands secrete,
> Vessels contract and expand
> At the right moment, essential fluids
> Flow to renew exhausted cells. . . .

I have implied that spirit is a power in you rather than being brought to you from outside. When Jesus was healing my foot, I claim that the passion and power of his spirit were in him. His spiritual experience was communicated to me in posture, "glowing," facial expression, timbre of voice, and in words. But the words were not the unbound, rational words which you are reading on this page. All of Jesus' communication was bound. His communication was only to my holistic, body-bound mind. In other words spirit is an internal pervasive power which is conscious-bound; it's hardly noticed. The spirit in you is the same, whether in a miraculous transcendence or the most mundane aspects of your everyday life.

Our rational culture assumes that spirit, if it is more than a superstition, is ethereal, a kind of celestial haze, far away from our everyday living.

But spirit is not an abstract, unbound concept of our rational minds; rather spirit is of our bodies, of the life of our bodies, of the evolution of our bodies. Spirit binds us to all of life, to its beginning and to its future. As the great German theologian Karl Rahner once said,

> The more I become my body, the more I become spirit; and the more I become spirit, the more I become my body.

The rational mind, idolatrously intent on preserving self-conscious identity, denies existence to whatever it can't control. Don't be surprised if it disputes the reality of body-bound spirit and makes it a rational spirit. "Rational" spirit is an innocuous idea, easily controlled, manipulated, and thus denied any independent reality.

The Binding of Spirit

I realize that what I have been about in my years of personal experimenting is to experience spirit intentionally through the will of my conscious mind. I didn't know that when I started. I have been trying to use methods of

personal scientific experimentation rather than the unex-
plainable inventions of artistic geniuses.

Then I began to realize that what makes humans unique
is their ability sometimes, very rarely, to transcend their
identities and be aware of their spirits with their rational
minds. It is only this rational mind, conscious of its own
functioning, unbound, which can rise above and self-consciously contemplate the spirit it cannot express, yearn for
the ultimate perfection of the spiritual qualities of love,
passion and sympathy from which this mind is alienated.
Let me say that again; it is so important to our understanding of the actuality of spirit: the unbound mind, with
its rational identity, feels awe when it can become conscious of the pure binding power of the spirit in the other
mind. The mental life binding the immortal cells of our
bodies is spirit.

Spirit *exists* only in the time-bound, body-bound, space-
bound world of evolution enfolding all of life from its very
beginnings. On the other hand it is only the rational mind,
conscious of its own functioning and forever alienated from
that world of life, which can *worship* spirit and make room
for it in our lives.

Spirit Does Not Fear Death
The bound mind knows all the body. Healing mind and
body are spiritually bound together sympathetically and

compassionately. Their work together is as perfect a love and freedom as four billion years of evolutionary binding can make it. Binding gives itself to living completely, without hesitation, all the way.

Think of standing near a loved one in a street. Imagine a speeding car about to run over this loved one.

ക്ക   ൦ൗ

What happened? There may have been two different things happening at the same time.

Did you in your imagination unhesitatingly rush to save this person? That was your healing spirit short-circuiting your rational identity and acting as George, the hunter in our example, acted, time-bound to his environment. If you stopped and thought about it before acting, that was your rational conscious identity. Both might have happened. Your identity is afraid of dying, afraid of rushing into the street unless goaded by rules of behavior. Your healing spirit is touched by an immortality unthinkably greater than your identity. Your bound self does not fear death and can sacrifice itself instantaneously.

Rational identity fears death because reason can only process information in a linear sequence. If the linear sequence is broken by death, there is nothing more.

However, your bound self only apprehends information as random, non-linear mental events. It cannot fear the ending of your rational mind's consciousness. The bound mind is not afraid of what is always immediate to its knowing. It lives with death in the cycles of life. Think of life as the history of beings dying and being born again, so as to change and grow.

When we die, the bound mental existence of our cells survives. Their cellular binding, the spirit, survives. And the bound mental existence of these cells has been changed forever by the way we have lived. Remember the binding power of love and compassion.

Do not forget your radiant body. Think of the difference between this radiance and your other, rational, mind. Your conscious mind and its cerebral computer operate logically, linearly and sequentially; neither exists except when it is in operation. On the other hand, your radiant healing mind has been living since life began. It is spiritual. The rational mind is of intellect. The bound healing mind is of spirit.

Our Culture and Spirit

Consider how foreign the existence of spirit is to our culture and our way of life. For instance, Descartes in the seventeenth century said *Cogito Ergo Sum,* "I think, therefore I am." I "think" is implicitly "I think rationally." The rest of the quotation is, "therefore I am." Who is the I? I is identity conscious of its own rational thinking. What

Descartes implicitly said was, "I think rationally, therefore I have identity—I am conscious of my own rational functioning." How radical and revolutionary this aphorism was. Philosophical existence was to depend on the rational mind.

Descartes could have said, "I love, therefore I am." He could have said, "I have precise emotional feeling tones, therefore I am," or, "I have spirit, therefore I am." What he did say, *Cogito Ergo Sum,* was the happy expression of the "Age of Reason," the rational child of the medieval rediscovery of Greek wisdom and rational mind's power, as I noted earlier. Descartes succinctly expressed the myth of what was to become our modern culture. The rational mind, conscious of itself, has come to occupy more and more of people's attention until the spiritual possibility of a revealed world has been all but forgotten.

Revelation

Spirit is revealed. The conscious-bound mind, one with its body and surroundings, is the door to the spirit. Since it is bound, its imagistic knowing and its lexicon can only be absolute. It cannot be relative. Revelation may be inappropriate; it can be wrong; but it can never be relative or rational.

While revelation is often defined in relation to the Bible, the Koran or other inspired writings, one does not expect to experience it within the contemporary religious context. Nevertheless, nonreligious revelation is quite common. To experience a revelation in church may be generally thought inappropriate or suspect; but if you go to church and would like to experiment with an unembarrassing revelation, try this:

Find a part of your worship service which you can say and which is the same every Sunday. Memorize it so you can say it comfortably. When the time comes to say it in church, let your rational mind idle. Let the congregation carry you along. You are not conscious of the words or what they mean even though you are saying them. Be aware of their cadence, feel the inexpressible flavor of communal worship. Let this rhythm and flavor carry you along to an emotional awareness of the act of worship repeating itself forever, past and future, all the souls who have participated and will participate. If that should happen, you would have experienced an absolute religious revelation. This revelation would be healing and would have occurred through the spiritual use of healing emotion and embodied words. Holloway said,

> Human kind has always "acted-out" all the moments that make life significant. We have an instinct for ceremony which owes its origin to the sacramental complexity of

reality. We are not just souls with bodies, we are embodied souls.

Loving Kindness

As human beings have long known, goodness and kindness are of the spirit and are saving. If you have loved and been loved in return, wasn't the spirit of that love more than your identity? Was it not outside of and free of the control of your reason? Doesn't that love remind you of the binding power of life, the spirit?

You may have read a story in *Time* magazine about child victims of the Far Eastern wars. These children had been collected in displaced persons camps in Hong Kong. Previously their families had been killed or lost. After that, they had wandered, subject to starvation and exposure, hunted by enemy soldiers seeking to kill or enslave them. But these few miraculously had survived.

A reporter interviewed many of these children to see if they had common qualities which might explain their survival. The common qualities he found were love, compassion, kindness and care for others. Similar qualities were found in those who survived the Nazi death camps. The body's ability to survive unhealthy conditions does not depend only on having a strong body but also a strong embodied spirit.

In the late second century St. Irenaus said it, "The glory

of God is a human person fully alive." For the ancient Christians, God's glory was two things: *revelation* and *presence*. Thus, to say "God reveals" is to say "God imparts himself, bestows himself." Revelation had nothing to do with information or facts, but with God's self-bestowal. *Revelation* is thus mutual *self-giving* (God's and ours).

The Spirit of the Body

Humankind during its long history has used many words for that which seems lost and also seems waiting: God, Goddess, Cosmic Mind, Universal Mind, Spirit. The experiments and personal research I have done seem to point in the direction of cosmic mind being just as real as human mind. The binding and enfolding of mind through time is the arrow I have taken the liberty of calling spirit. My experience, and it's only my experience, suggests that this arrow points in the direction of something pervasive and cosmic which is always in the process of becoming. My assumption would be that this pervasive mental flux would accumulate around our planet in a mental well similar to the gravity well in which we live. This focus of life would be what we have called our biosphere.

I mention such speculations to make clear the bias with which I approached the tentative experimental direction which follows. First, since the experiments recounted in this book had not led to a rational reconciliation between the two minds, then perhaps transcendence would be a fruitful direction. Perhaps the alienation between body-bound mind and rational, conscious mind would disappear in the passion of spirit.

I have described many paths to living fully with all one is and can be. In my own attempts to reach a final research design, I proposed letting these ways all become transcended in healing spirit. I decided I could only keep of my life what my identity could give up. I attempted to let the passion of spirit turn away the rules, systems and shoulds of my identity-centeredness.

So how to start? I went back over the personal scientific experiments which became this book to be sure I had assimilated them thoroughly. Remember, in the first three chapters we experimented with the possibilities of having a mind and then the possibilities of having a mind separate from the one which seemed to be the only one we had.

The fourth chapter began experiments of communication with that other mind through the imagistic space of dreams. These experiences were of a primal world still existing within us in parallel with our rational mind.

In the fifth chapter we experimented with standing and with walking or jogging as the "graces of space." Some of these experiments of spatial grace hopefully became a part of our living. This grace is also a part of that primal world which existed before the evolution of the rational mind and still exists as an aspect of the other mind.

Then we experimented with bonding images to those personal surroundings which are normally dominated by rational mind. These bondings were to derationalize personal surroundings in a passive way.

On the other hand, bonding words in the seventh chapter was an experiment aimed at actively derationalizing focused intentions so we could live fully and all the way. It was a further step towards bringing our other mind into a full partnership in our life. I tested each of these routines to be sure they had actually provided me with workable keys to my imaginal mind, keys which I actively used in everyday living.

Finally, I tested the healing powers of rationally controlling my behavior while simultaneously releasing my emotions to be fully experienced. In that experiment I was no longer derationalizing my experiences but finally using my two minds together freely and fully. Then I began to feel my lifetime accumulation of repressed emotions beginning to be assimilated in that which encompasses all life. That is where I am still working.

I had attempted to be subjectively rigorous in these experiments and being truly rigorous meant going no further until I had carried the emotional experiments as far as they would go. However, I also felt and feel that to go further I need help.

We can help each other. So with that assurance I went ahead with the tentative design for this chapter. What I had helping me were the gradual inner processes that had been going on within me during those years of writing this book. I had hardly noticed the changes, but when I came to this experimental impasse, I realized I hadn't been doing experiments; they had been doing me. What does it mean when every experiment I do to find the full truth of myself changes me as part of the result of the experiment? The Nobel Laureates I have mentioned, who have written *Nobel Prize Conversations,* seem to have had to ask the same question when they approached the limiting edge of physical knowledge.

Spiritual Non-Experiment

We have experienced various aspects of spirit in this book. We have had an opportunity to discover if we were being misled by those experiences. Remember, science doesn't need to be rational or conscious of itself. What science must be is a method to help us keep from being misled by our experiences.

I discovered I could now cash in on an effort I had put into the record of the experiments I had been keeping. I went back to the experiments which had become my experience of being fully alive. I searched through them for bound-to-body word keys and body-image-in-space keys which had to do with family, lovers and friends in the context of healing, love, compassion, kindness and sympathy. I made a list of them as an addition to my record.

In the coming experiment, these were the surroundings through which I would drift. I let them spread all through me; let myself glow until one of these experiences had become merged into a transcendent feeling tone of the binding spirit itself.

If spirit didn't come, I let go and started another time. When it did happen, and it would happen in a blink, I knew it. I had a feeling tone of the passion of spiritual binding itself, free of word, image or emotion. I let this feeling tone seep into my living.

If you have had similar experiences, I hope the feeling tone will become a transcendent door for your own future experiments through which you will go deeper into your spirit. Keep going. This is a purifying process which should lead back through time. You are no longer trying to break through the rational mind to reach your healing mind. You are transcending your rational mind with love and joy. And you'll discover that the answer to the old Zen quotation about "the sound of one hand clapping" is knee-slapping laughter or a crack on the head from the Zen master's staff. There is no rational answer.

This process may take weeks, months, years. Hopefully, you will find better experimental designs. At some point you may transcend your experiences of dream, surroundings, image, word and emotion, to live all in one spiritual pattern of being fully alive.

Perhaps when you touch this immortal spiritual unity, you will find that your *efforts* to try to live fully have dropped away. Vital living with all you are may be revealed as just a by-product of the passion of your pure opened-up spirit. This would be a new kind of knowing.

But do not be misled. It is important for you to come to these experimental beginnings only by your own personal research. However, to go on alone is not easy. Continue these experiments with others. That is not easy either. The truly disastrous way is to form a group for the purpose of seeking a fuller life. In that case you will inevitably find that your rational identity has locked itself up with other ravenous identities. Healing, freedom and spirit will all become rational charades.

You cannot control or direct or manipulate the others who can share this quest. The answer is simple. Be comfortable with your spiritual healing mind in personal confidence and inner power. If there is anyone else like that around, you will know each other. Another old Zen master once said, "This cannot be taught; it can be known only by rubbing two people together."

Spiritual Journey

The spirit is a total way of being in the world which may reorient an ill way of being in the world to a transcendent healing path of love, compassion and joy.

Ernest Haycox put it well,

> . . . . the world turned over, it meant the difference between living and non-living, the difference between light and dark, cold and heat. It meant a full heart, a wild, strange, and ever-changing feeling, it meant all the colors and all the sounds, it meant a thousand unexpressed thoughts; it meant taking and giving, it meant feelings that ran all the way from rich goodness to cruelty; all things full and nothing empty.

A full life means being bound in harmony with body, surroundings and all the interacting life of our planet. It exists from the beginning of all life. This spiritual binding is our touch of immortality.

Will rational psychological rules and sectarian systems

save you? You know in your heart they will not. The most you can do is live in harmony with your surroundings and to live in passion and excitement with others who can live the same way. Your spirit depends on the spirit of all life.

It is so easy to think of spiritual living as being relaxation and rest. But that is not to be fully alive. Spirit is passion and power. It is serenity and purity. Serenity of spirit is not relaxation. Purity is not peace. Serenity is a vivid kind of living in harmony with the whole biosphere. Purity is the scientific quest you have followed in this book. It is a method which is demanding and disciplined. It is like dying to your old self and being reborn.

We have come on a strange circular journey to the shores of a new continent of mind. I can only show you the line of waves breaking on that dark shore. We must each do our own exploring. We must each find our own true self and know for the first time our whole spirit, bright and clean, full of passion and life.

Write me care of Saybrook Publishing Company.
Remember, we're all in the same boat.
We need each other.

Tom's Record
October 15

Took cigarette to sales meeting. Blew smoke in Peter's face. Delighted as he sputtered. Found myself getting up and embracing him. Both laughed. We really are friends as well as enemies. Cigarette at lunch tasted so good. Find I'm getting down to one after lunch and one after dinner. Lunch good too, but think I'm losing weight. Eating less?

Driving home, air zingy, me zingy. How many times have I done the spiritual exercise, four, five? That feeling was swelling up. Out of traffic— parked on side street. Sat back and let it happen. No shifts like before—just bam and back at the old house where I grew up—like it was. Walked around it. Then back towards garage. There I was sitting hunched against back wall, little kid about six. He—I—looked up at me so accusingly—big broody eyes. My heart broke. I held out my arms with everything I had—He came—not into my arms—into me. Something happened.

Kids and I sang John's school song at dinner, making Mary mad. But O.K.

Decided after dinner to stop this record. It's not doing anything for me anymore. Think it's keeping me into myself when everything in me wants to flow out. After tonight, good-bye record—with love—all the way.

After everyone in bed we had Love, Bliss. Love her all night long—maybe most when asleep. Turning in now. Good night, record. Next week last session— Good—I've had it.

Dream—bright green grass—dark green trees at edges—G.W.'s statue—park—flight of pure white pigeons took off from green up in air in one fluid moment and leaders down before the last took off. Sky blue— fluffy clouds—no movement—no people—no wind—just that pattern of flight etched against the sky.

THE GLORY OF GOD
IS A HUMAN BEING FULLY ALIVE
                    Saint Irenaus of Lyons
                        Second Century.

ACKNOWLEDGMENTS

Grateful acknowledgment is made for permission to quote:

CHAPTER ONE

The lines from "The Road Not Taken" from *The Poetry of Robert Frost* by Robert Frost, edited by Edward Connery Lathem. Reprinted by permission of Holt, Rinehart and Winston, Inc. Copyright © 1969 by Holt, Rinehart and Winston, Inc.

The lines from *"The Optimist's Daughter,* by Eudora Welty. Reprinted by permission of Random House, Inc. Copyright © 1969, 1972 by Eudora Welty.

The lines from "The Odor of Rosemary," by Glenway Wescott, from *Perfected Steel, Terrible Crystal.* An Unconventional Source Book of Spiritual Readings in Poetry and Prose, by Ned O'Gorman. New York: The Seabury Press, 1981. Copyright © 1981 by Ned O'Gorman.

The lines from "The Starlight Night" from *Poems of Gerard Manley Hopkins,* by Gerard M. Hopkins. Reprinted by permission of Oxford University Press. Copyright © 1953, 1966 by Oxford University Press.

CHAPTER TWO

The lines from "Sonnet to Orpheus" from *Selected Poems of Rainer Maria Rilke,* by R. M. Rilke, translated with commentary by Robert Bly. Reprinted by permission of Harper & Row, Publishers, Inc. Copyright © 1981 by Robert Bly.

The lines from "Children of Adam" from *Poetry and Prose* by Walt Whitman, edited by Justin Kaplan. Reprinted by permission of The Library of America. Copyright © 1982 by Literary Classics of the United States, Inc.

The lines from "The Dry Salvages" from *Four Quartets,* by T. S. Eliot. Reprinted by permission of Harcourt Brace Jovanovich, Inc. Copyright © 1958, 1962 by T. S. Eliot; renewed 1971 by Esme Valery Eliot.

CHAPTER THREE

The lines from "Horae Canonicae" from *W. H. Auden: Collected Poems,* by W. H. Auden, edited by Edward Mendelson. Reprinted by permission of Random House, Inc. Copyright © 1960, 1965, 1969, 1972 by W. H. Auden; renewed 1975 by Edward Mendelson, William Meredith and Monroe K. Spears, executors of the estate of W. H. Auden. Cited also in chapters Four and Nine.

The lines from "Genesis," and other biblical quotations in this book, from the *Holy Bible: New International Version.* Used by permission of Zondervan Bible Publishers. Copyright © 1973, 1978 by the International Bible Society.

CHAPTER FOUR

The lines from Ursula K. LeGuin, excerpted from *The Lathe of Heaven.* Copyright © 1971 Ursula K. LeGuin. Reprinted with permission of Charles Scribner's Sons.

The lines from "Sunday Morning" from *The Collected Poems of Wallace Stevens,* by Wallace Stevens. Reprinted by permission of Alfred Knopf, Inc. Copyright © 1954 by Wallace Stevens.

CHAPTER FIVE

The lines from the Papago Indian "Dream Song" from *In the Trail of the Wind,* by John Bierhorst. Reprinted by permission of Farrar, Straus and Giroux, Inc. Copyright © 1971 by John Bierhorst.

CHAPTER SIX

CHAPTER SEVEN

The lines from "Archaic Torso of Apollo" from *Selected Poems of Rainer Maria Rilke,* by R. M. Rilke, translated, with commentary, by Robert Bly. Reprinted by permission of Harper and Row, Publishers, Inc. Copyright © 1981 by Robert Bly.

CHAPTER EIGHT

The lines from Ursula K. LeGuin, excerpted from *The Farthest Shore.* Copyright © 1972 Ursula K. LeGuin. Reprinted with the permission of Atheneum Publishers.

The lines from "Sailing to Byzantium" from *The Poems of W. B. Yeats,* by W. B. Yeats, edited by Richard J. Finneran. Reprinted by permission of Macmillan Publishing Company. Copyright © 1928 by Macmillan Publishing Company, Inc., renewed 1956 by Georgie Yeats.

CHAPTER NINE

The lines from "Less and Less Human, O Savage Spirit" from *The Collected Poems of Wallace Stevens,* by Wallace Stevens. Reprinted by permission of Alfred A. Knopf, Inc. Copyright © 1954 by Wallace Stevens.